# BE

## REAL

# BE

## REAL

### TURNING FROM HYPOCRISY TO TRUTH

## NT COMMENTARY

## 1 JOHN

# Warren W. Wiersbe

transforming lives together

BE REAL
Published by David C Cook
4050 Lee Vance View
Colorado Springs, CO 80918 U.S.A.

David C Cook Distribution Canada
55 Woodslee Avenue, Paris, Ontario, Canada N3L 3E5

David C Cook U.K., Kingsway Communications
Eastbourne, East Sussex BN23 6NT, England

The graphic circle C logo is a registered trademark of David C Cook.

Unless otherwise noted, all Scripture quotations are taken from the King James Version
of the Bible. (Public Domain.) Scripture quotations marked NASB are taken from the *New
American Standard Bible*, © Copyright 1960, 1995 by The Lockman Foundation. Used
by permission; PH are taken from J. B. Phillips: *The New Testament in Modern English*,
revised editions © J. B. Phillips, 1958, 1960, 1972, permission of Macmillan Publishing
Co. and Collins Publishers; SCO are taken from the New Scofield Reference Bible, King
James version, © 1967 by Oxford University Press, Inc. Reprinted by permission; and
NIV are taken from the *Holy Bible, New International Version*®. *NIV*®. Copyright ©
1973, 1978, 1984 by International Bible Society. Used by permission of Zondervan. All
rights reserved. The author has added italics in Scripture quotations for emphasis.

LCCN 2009923016
ISBN 978-1-4347-6744-8
eISBN 978-1-4347-0024-7

© 1972 Warren W. Wiersbe

First edition of *Be Real* by Warren W. Wiersbe published by Victor Books®
in 1972 © Warren W. Wiersbe, ISBN 978-0-89693-774-1

The Team: Karen Lee-Thorp, Amy Kiechlin, Jack Campbell, and Susan Vannaman
Series Cover Design: John Hamilton Design
Cover Photo: Veer Images

Printed in the United States of America
Second Edition 2009

7 8 9 10

012815

*To Dr. Howard F. Sugden*
*Devoted Pastor/Gifted Expositor/Beloved Friend*

# CONTENTS

# THE BIG IDEA

## An Introduction to *Be Real*
## by Ken Baugh

I was having dinner one night with my family, and somehow our conversation landed on the topic of the end times. You know—the end-of-the-world stuff, Revelation, armageddon, plagues, death, earthquakes, famine, pestilence—your basic end-of-life-on-planet-earth-as-we-know-it scenario. As we were talking, my oldest daughter reminded me of a conversation she and I had years ago. She was afraid of dying because she wasn't 100 percent certain that she was saved. She confessed that night at dinner that even though she has asked Jesus Christ into her life to forgive her sin and be her Savior, she still became a little fearful as to whether or not her salvation was real when the topic of death was brought up.

The truth is there have been times even in my own life when I have been afraid of the same thing. How about you? Are you 100 percent convinced that if you were to have a fatal heart attack in the next two minutes while reading this, you would go to heaven? Really think about it for a second: How do you know that if you were to die right now you would go to heaven?

If you are getting a bit queasy like my daughter, you're reading the right commentary, because the reason John wrote this letter was to give every believer the ability to evaluate the reality of their faith and to be confident in their salvation. John wants you to have absolute, 100 percent confidence in regard to your salvation. This is the Big Idea that runs throughout his letter. Look what he says: "I write these things to you who believe in the name of the Son of God so that you may know that you have eternal life" (1 John 5:13 NIV). So what evidence does John point to that reveals true, saving faith? Let's take a look.

First, I know that I am truly saved if I have confessed my sin to God. John says, "If we claim to be without sin, we deceive ourselves and the truth is not in us. If we confess our sins, he is faithful and just and will forgive us our sins and purify us from all unrighteousness" (1:8–9 NIV). The way to confess your sin is simply to pray, saying something like this: "Lord Jesus, I believe I am a sinner and that my sin has separated me from you. Please forgive me of all my sin, cleanse my heart from all unrighteousness, and be my Lord and Savior. Amen." If you prayed that prayer or one like it, you can know with confidence that your sin has been forgiven because John tells us that if we confess, God forgives. That's good news!

Second, I know that I am truly saved if I obey Jesus' commands. John makes it clear that obedience is partial evidence that a person is truly saved: "We know that we have come to know him if we obey his commands" (2:3 NIV); "This is how we know who the children of God are and who the children of the devil are: Anyone who does not do what is right is not a child of God …" (3:10 NIV); and "We know that anyone born of God does not continue to sin …" (5:18 NIV). John emphasizes that a true believer lives a life of obedience to the commands of the Lord Jesus.

Now, that doesn't mean that I can obey perfectly all the time, because John tells us, "If we claim to be without sin, we deceive ourselves and the truth is not in us" (1:8 NIV). We all sin, even as true believers. The issue isn't perfect obedience where we never falter, but rather a desire to obey Jesus' commands that manifests itself through consistency. Perfection isn't going to come this side of heaven. So if you have the desire to live a life of obedience, that's a good sign that you're truly saved. However, if you have no desire to obey the commands of Jesus, no desire to live a righteous life, and no conviction by the Holy Spirit when you do sin, you should question whether or not you are truly saved. True salvation manifests itself in a heartfelt desire to obey and a broken heart when you don't. These are sure indications of genuine salvation.

Third, I know that I am truly saved if I believe that Jesus Christ came to earth some two thousand years ago as God in human flesh. John says, "Everyone who believes that Jesus is the Christ is born of God" (5:1 NIV). I demonstrate true evidence of salvation through faith that Jesus and Jesus alone is the "only true God" (John 17:3 NIV), who came and walked among us (1:41). In addition, I must believe that Jesus was the only one who could die in my place to pay the price for my sin as the perfect "Lamb of God who takes away the sin of the world" (1:29 NIV)—and that He is the only way to heaven (14:6). If you believe these things, you can be assured that you have genuine faith and are truly saved.

Fourth, I know that I am truly saved if I love other believers. True saving faith manifests itself in a sincere love for other believers. John says, "Anyone who does not do what is right is not a child of God; nor is anyone who does not love his brother" (1 John 3:10 NIV). Love is so much more than feelings expressed through words. True love is manifested through action: "Let us not love with words or tongue but with actions and in truth" (3:18 NIV).

But what type of action demonstrates the true state of my salvation, you ask? Good question. Simply put, we are to love one another in the same way that Jesus loved us: sacrificially and unconditionally. "Everyone who loves has been born of God and knows God.… This is how God showed his love among us: He sent his one and only Son into the world that we might live through him" (4:7, 9 NIV). We show love to one another when we make sacrifices to help them in times of need, and we love others unconditionally when we help them with no strings attached. For example, if they are in need of clothing, we clothe them. If they need food, we feed them. If they need money, we give it to them. This is not some type of Christian welfare system, because the Bible tells us that everyone who can work must do their part (see 2 Thess. 3:6–15). Instead, when something happens in a person's life—they lose their job, they injure themselves, or whatever—we as Christians are to come to their aid. As we help other believers in times of need, we demonstrate that we are authentic children of God: "Whoever loves God must also love his brother" (1 John 4:21 NIV). So if you actively love others, that's another piece of evidence that you are truly saved.

These are the four elements that reveal true saving faith. Now, one last thing: I want to make sure that you don't think I'm some type of works-oriented, legalistic pastor. I believe that we are saved by grace through faith, not works (Eph. 2:8–9). That is the clear teaching of the Bible. But I also believe the Bible teaches that genuine faith will demonstrate itself through the beliefs and behaviors that I stated above. Remember the words of James: "Faith by itself, if it is not accompanied by action, is dead" (James 2:17). Therefore, the real believer, the person who should have 100 percent confidence in their salvation—that when they die they will go to heaven—is the person whose faith leads to action and whose actions are motivated by faith. I pray that as you read through this commentary, you will not only experience the blessed assurance of your own salvation, but you will also be able to help other believers who might be struggling with doubt about their own.

***

Dr. Wiersbe's commentaries have been a source of guidance and strength to me over the many years that I have been a pastor. His unique style is theologically sound but not overly academic. He explains the deep truths of Scripture in a way that everyone can understand and apply. Whether you're a Bible scholar or a brand-new believer in Christ, you will benefit, as I have, from Warren's insights. With your Bible in one hand and Dr. Wiersbe's commentary in the other, you will be able to unpack the deep truths of God's Word accurately and learn how to apply them to your life.

Drink deeply, my friend, of the truths of God's Word, for in them you will find Jesus Christ, and there is freedom, peace, assurance, and joy.

—Ken Baugh
Pastor of Coast Hills Community Church
Aliso Viejo, California

# A Word from Robert A. Cook

Warren Wiersbe has managed to work into his book *Be Real* all the things for which his friends remember and appreciate him. Wiersbe is noted for his phrasing and choice of words. He will not disappoint you here. He comes through with expressions that will delight the heart of anyone interested in enlarging his horizons of expression.

Wiersbe stands for good, wholesome humor, even whimsy at times. One has the feeling that one who can smile at the human race—including himself—will never be in danger of getting stuffy.

Those who know him best know that Warren Wiersbe never fails to lead his hearers and readers straight to a confrontation with the will of God. This is first and last and always a man committed to doing God's will. He never lets you forget it.

Wiersbe's writing does for prose what the apostle Paul thought should be done for singing and praying: "I will pray with the spirit, and I will pray with the understanding also: I will sing with the spirit, and I will sing with the understanding also" (1 Cor. 14:15).

This author blesses you. One can feel in heart and conscience the touch of God's Holy Spirit as the pages turn; but Warren Wiersbe makes you think, too! Here is no neatly packaged, predigested religious cereal: Here is Bible truth, clearly explained and faithfully applied.

Go ahead, read it … help yourself to a blessing, and *Be Real*!

—Robert A. Cook, former president of
The King's College, Briarcliff Manor, N.Y.

# A Suggested Outline of the Book of 1 John

Theme: The tests of reality in the Christian life

Key verse: 1 John 5:13

I. Introduction (1 John 1:1–4)

II. The Tests of True Fellowship: God Is Light (1 John 1:5—2:29)

    A. Obedience (1 John 1:5—2:6) ("saying" versus "doing")

    B. Love (1 John 2:7–17)

    C. Truth (1 John 2:18–29)

III. The Tests of True Sonship: God Is Love (1 John 3—5)

    A. Obedience (1 John 3)

    B. Love (1 John 4)

    C. Truth (1 John 5)

# Chapter One

# IT'S REAL!

## (1 John 1:1–4)

O nce upon a time …" Remember how exciting those words used to be? They were the open door into an exciting world of make-believe, a dreamworld that helped you forget all the problems of childhood.

Then—pow! You turned a corner one day, and "Once upon a time" became kid stuff. You discovered that life is a battleground, not a playground, and fairy stories were no longer meaningful. You wanted something real.

The search for something real is not new. It has been going on since the beginning of history. Men have looked for reality and satisfaction in wealth, thrills, conquest, power, learning, and even in religion.

There is nothing really wrong with these experiences, except that by themselves they never really satisfy. Wanting something real and finding something real are two different things. Like a child eating cotton candy at the circus, many people who expect to bite into something real end up with a mouthful of nothing. They waste priceless years on empty substitutes for reality.

This is where the apostle John's first epistle comes in. Written centuries ago, this letter deals with a theme that is forever up-to-date: the life that is real.

John had discovered that satisfying reality is not to be found in things or thrills, but in a Person—Jesus Christ, the Son of God. Without wasting any time, he told us about this "living reality" in the first paragraph of his letter.

As you read 1 John 1:1–4, you learn three vital facts about the life that is real.

## 1. THIS LIFE IS REVEALED (1:1)

As you read John's letter, you will discover that he enjoyed using certain words and that the word *manifest* is one of them. "For the life was manifested" (1 John 1:2), he said. This life was not hidden so that we have to search for it and find it. No, it was manifested—revealed openly!

If you were God, how would you go about revealing yourself to men? How could you tell them about, and give them, the kind of life you wanted them to enjoy?

God has revealed Himself in creation (Rom. 1:20), but creation alone could never tell us the story of God's love. God has also revealed Himself much more fully in His Word, the Bible. But God's final and most complete revelation is in His Son, Jesus Christ. Jesus said, "He that hath seen me hath seen the Father" (John 14:9).

Because Jesus is God's revelation of Himself, He has a very special name: "The Word of life" (1 John 1:1).

This same title opens John's gospel: "In the beginning was the Word, and the Word was with God, and the Word was God" (John 1:1).

Why does Jesus Christ have this name? Because Christ is to us what our words are to others. Our words reveal to others just what we think and how we feel. Christ reveals to us the mind and heart of God. He is the living means of communication between God and men. To know Jesus Christ is to know God!

John made no mistake in his identification of Jesus Christ. Jesus is the Son of the Father—the Son of God (1 John 1:3). John warned us several times in his letter not to listen to the false teachers who tell lies about Jesus Christ. "Who is a liar but he that denieth that Jesus is the Christ?" (2:22). "Every spirit that confessed that Jesus Christ is come in the flesh is of God; and every spirit that confesseth not that Jesus Christ is come in the flesh is not of God" (4:2–3). If a man is wrong about Jesus Christ, he is wrong about God, because Jesus Christ is the final and complete revelation of God to men.

For example, there are those who tell us that Jesus was a man but was not God. John had no place for such teachers! One of the last things he wrote in this letter is "We are in him that is true, even in his Son Jesus Christ This is the true God, and eternal life" (1 John 5:20).

False teaching is so serious a matter that John wrote about it in his second letter too, warning believers not to invite false teachers into their homes (2 John 9–10). And he made it plain that to deny that Jesus is God is to follow the lies of the antichrist (1 John 2:22–23).

This leads to a basic Bible doctrine that has puzzled many people—the doctrine of the Trinity.

John mentioned in his letter the Father, the Son, and the Holy Spirit. For example, he said, "By this know ye the Spirit of God: every spirit that confesseth that Jesus Christ is come in the flesh is of God" (1 John 4:2 SCO). Here are references in one verse to God the Father, God the Son, and God the Holy Spirit. And in 1 John 4:13–15 is another statement that mentions the three Persons of the Trinity.

The word *trinity* is a combination of tri-, meaning "three," and unity, meaning "one." A "trinity," then, is a three-in-one, or one-in-three. To be sure, the word *trinity* is not found in the Bible, but the truth is taught there (cf. also Matt. 28:19–20; John 14:16–17, 26; 2 Cor. 13:14; Eph. 4:4–6).

Christians do not believe that there are three gods. They believe that one God exists in three Persons—Father, Son, and Holy Spirit. Nor do Christians believe merely that one God reveals Himself in three different ways, much as one man may be a husband, a father, and a son. No, the Bible teaches that God is one but that He exists in three Persons.

One teacher of doctrine used to say, "Try to explain the Trinity and you may lose your mind. But try to explain it away and you will lose your soul!" And the apostle John says, "Whoever denies the Son does not have the Father" (1 John 2:23 NASB). No Person of the Trinity is expendable!

As you read the gospel records of the life of Jesus, you see the wonderful kind of life God wants us to enjoy. But it is not by imitating Jesus, our example, that we may share in this life. No, there is a far better way.

## 2. THIS LIFE IS EXPERIENCED (1:2)

Read the first four verses of John's letter again, and you will notice that the apostle had a personal encounter with Jesus Christ. His was no second-hand "religious experience" inherited from somebody else or discovered in a book! No, John knew Jesus Christ face-to-face. He and the other apostles heard Jesus speak. They watched Him as He lived with them. In fact, they studied Him carefully, and even touched His body. They knew that Jesus was real—not a phantom, not a vision, but God in human corporeal form.

Some twenty-first-century student may say, "Yes, and this means that John had an advantage. He lived when Jesus walked on earth. He knew Jesus personally. But I was born twenty centuries too late!"

But this is where our student is wrong! It was not the apostles' physical nearness to Jesus Christ that made them what they were. It was their spiritual nearness. They had committed themselves to Him as their Savior and their Lord. Jesus Christ was real and exciting to John and his colleagues because they had trusted Him. By trusting Christ, they had experienced eternal life!

Six times in this letter John used the phrase "born of God." This was not an idea John had invented; he had heard Jesus use these words. "Except a man be born again," Jesus had said, "he cannot see the kingdom of God.... That which is born of the flesh is flesh; and that which is born of the Spirit is spirit. Marvel not that I said unto thee, Ye must be born again" (John 3:3, 6–7). We can experience this "real life" only after we have believed the gospel, put our trust in Christ, and been "born of God."

"Whosoever believeth that Jesus is the Christ is born of God" (1 John 5:1). Eternal life is not something we earn by good works or deserve because of good character. Eternal life, the life that is real, is a gift from God to those who trust His Son as their Savior.

John wrote his gospel to tell people how to receive this wonderful life (John 20:31). He wrote his first letter to tell people how to be sure they have really been born of God (1 John 5:9–13).

A college student returned to the campus after going home for a family funeral, and almost at once his grades began to go down. His counselor thought that the death of his grandmother had affected the boy and that time would heal the wound, but the grades only became worse. Finally the boy confessed the real problem. While he was home, he happened to look into his grandmother's old Bible, and there he discovered in the family record that he was an adopted son.

"I don't know who I belong to," he told his counselor. "I don't know where I came from!"

The assurance that we are in God's family—that we have been "born of God"—is vitally important to all of us. Certain characteristics are true of all God's children. A person who is born of God lives a righteous life (1 John 2:29). A child of God does not practice sin (which is the meaning of the King James word *commit*, 1 John 3:9). A believer will occasionally commit sin (cf. 1 John 1:8—2:2), but he will not make it a habit to sin.

God's children also love one another and their heavenly Father (cf.

1 John 4:7; 5:1). They have no love for the world system around them (2:15–17), and because of this the world hates them (3:13). Instead of being overcome by the pressures of this world and swept off balance, the children of God overcome the world (5:4). This is another mark of true children of God.

Why is it so important that we know that we have been born of God? John gives us the answer: If you are not a child of God, you a "child of wrath" (Eph. 2:1–3) and may become a "child of the devil" (1 John 3:10; and see Matt: 13:24–30, 36–43). A "child of the devil" is a counterfeit Christian who acts "saved" but has not been born again. Jesus called the Pharisees "children of the devil" (John 8:44), and they were very religious.

A counterfeit Christian—and they are common—is something like a counterfeit ten-dollar bill.

Suppose you have a counterfeit bill and actually think it is genuine. You use it to pay for a tank of gas. The gas station manager uses the bill to buy supplies. The supplier uses the bill to pay the grocer. The grocer bundles the bill up with forty-nine other ten-dollar bills and takes it to the bank. And the teller says, "I'm sorry, but this bill is a counterfeit."

That ten-dollar bill may have done a lot of good while it was in circulation, but when it arrived at the bank, it was exposed for what it really was and pulled out of circulation.

So with a counterfeit Christian. He may do many good things in this life, but when he faces the final judgment he will be rejected. "Many will say to me in that day, Lord, Lord, have we not prophesied in thy name? And in thy name have cast out demons? And in thy name done many wonderful works? And then will I profess unto them, I never knew you; depart from me, ye that work iniquity" (Matt. 7:22–23 SCO).

Each of us must ask himself honestly, "Am I a true child of God, or am I a counterfeit Christian? Have I truly been born of God?"

If you have not experienced eternal life, this real life, you can experience it right now! Read 1 John 5:9–15 carefully. God has "gone on record" in His Word. He offers you the gift of eternal life. Believe His promise and ask Him for His gift. "For whosoever shall call upon the name of the Lord shall be saved" (Rom. 10:13).

We have discovered two important facts about "the life that is real": It is revealed in Jesus Christ, and it is experienced when we put our trust in Him as our Savior. But John did not stop here!

### 3. THIS LIFE IS SHARED (1:3–4)

"That which we have seen and heard declare we unto you" (1 John 1:3). And once you have experienced this exciting life that is real, you will want to share it with other people, just as John wanted to "declare" it to all his readers in the first century.

A pastor had a phone call from an angry woman. "I have received a piece of religious literature from your church," she shouted, "and I resent your using the mail to upset people!"

"What was so upsetting about a piece of mail from a church?" the pastor asked calmly.

"You have no right to try to change my religion!" the woman stormed. "You have your religion and I have mine, and I'm not trying to change yours!" (She really was, but the pastor didn't argue with her.)

"Changing your religion, or anybody else's religion, is not our purpose," the pastor explained. "But we have experienced a wonderful new life through faith in Christ, and we want to do all we can to share it with others."

Many people (including some Christians) have the idea that "witnessing" means wrangling over the differences in religious beliefs or sitting down and comparing churches.

That isn't what John had in mind! He told us that witnessing means sharing our spiritual experiences with others—both by the lives that we live and by the words that we speak.

John wrote this letter to share Christ with us. As you read it, you will discover that John had in mind five purposes for sharing.

**(1) That we may have fellowship (v. 3).** This word *fellowship* is an important one in the vocabulary of a Christian. It simply means "to have in common." As sinners, men have nothing in common with the holy God. But God in His grace sent Christ to have something in common with men. Christ took on Himself a human body and became a man. Then He went to the cross and took on that body the sins of the world (1 Peter 2:24). Because He paid the price for our sins, the way is open for God to forgive us and take us into His family. When we trust Christ, we become "partakers of the divine nature" (2 Peter 1:4). The term translated "partakers" in Peter's epistle is from the same Greek root that is translated "fellowship" in 1 John 1:3.

What a thrilling miracle! Jesus Christ took on Himself the nature of man that by faith we may receive the very nature of God! A famous British writer was leaving Liverpool by ship. He noticed that the other passengers were waving to friends on the dock. He rushed down to the dock and stopped a little boy. "Would you wave to me if I paid you?" he asked the lad, and of course the boy agreed. The writer rushed back on board and leaned over the rail, glad for someone to wave to. And sure enough, there was the boy waving back to him!

A foolish story? Perhaps—but it reminds us that man hates loneliness. All of us want to be wanted. The life that is real helps to solve the basic problem of loneliness, for Christians have genuine fellowship with God and with one another. Jesus promised, "Lo, I am with you always" (Matt. 28:20). In his letter, John explained the secret of fellowship with God and with other Christians. This is the first purpose John mentioned for the writing of his letter—the sharing of his experience of eternal life.

**(2) That we may have joy (v. 4).** Fellowship is Christ's answer to the loneliness of life. Joy is His answer to the emptiness, the hollowness, of life.

John, in his epistle, used the word joy only once, but the idea of joy runs through the entire letter. Joy is not something that we manufacture for ourselves; joy is a wonderful by-product of our fellowship with God. David knew the joy that John mentioned; he said, "In thy presence is fullness of joy" (Ps. 16:11).

Basically, sin is the cause of the unhappiness that overwhelms our world today. Sin promises joy, but it always produces sorrow. The pleasures of sin are temporary—they are only for a season (Heb. 11:25). God's pleasures last eternally—they are forevermore (Ps. 16:11).

The life that is real produces a joy that is real—not some limp substitute. Jesus said, the night before He was crucified, "Your joy no man taketh from you" (John 16:22). "These things have I spoken unto you, that my joy might remain in you, and that your joy might be full" (15:11).

Karl Marx wrote, "The first requisite for the people's happiness is the abolition of religion." But the apostle John wrote, in effect, "Faith in Jesus Christ gives you a joy that can never be duplicated by the world. I have experienced this joy myself, and I want to share it with you."

**(3) That we may not sin (2:1).** John faced the problem of sin squarely (cf. 1 John 3:4–9, for example) and announced the only answer to this enigma—the Person and work of Jesus Christ. Christ not only died for us to carry the penalty of our sins, but rose from the dead in order to intercede for us at the throne of God: "If any man sin, we have an advocate with the Father, Jesus Christ the righteous" (1 John 2:1).

Christ is our Representative. He defends us at the Father's throne. Satan may stand there as the accuser of the brethren (Zech. 3; Rev. 12:10), but Christ stands there as our Advocate—He pleads on our behalf! Continuing forgiveness, in response to His intercession, is God's answer to our sinfulness.

"I would like to become a Christian," an interested woman said to a visiting pastor, "but I'm afraid I can't hold out. I'm sure to sin again!"

Turning to 1 John 1, the pastor said, "No doubt you will sin again, because God says, 'If we say that we have no sin, we deceive ourselves, and the truth is not in us' (1 John 1:8). But if you do sin, God will forgive you if you will confess your sin to Him. But it isn't necessary for Christians to sin. As we walk in fellowship with God and in obedience to His Word, He gives us ability to resist and to have victory over temptation."

Then the pastor remembered that the woman had gone through surgery some months before.

"When you had your surgery," he asked, "was there a possibility of complications or problems afterward?"

"Oh, yes," she replied. "But whenever I had a problem, I went to see the doctor and he took care of it."

Then the truth hit her! "I see it!" she exclaimed. "Christ is always available to keep me out of sin or to forgive my sin!"

The life that is real is a life of victory. In this letter, John told us how to draw on our divine resources to experience victory over temptation and sin.

**(4) That we may not be deceived (2:26).** As never before, Christians today need ability to distinguish between right and wrong, between truth and error. The notion is widespread in our generation that there are no "absolutes"—that nothing is always wrong and that nothing is always right. False doctrines, therefore, are more prevalent than at any time in history—and most men and women seem to be willing to accept almost any teaching except the truths of the Bible.

In John's epistles is a word that no other New Testament writer uses—*antichrist* (1 John 2:18, 22; 4:3; 2 John 7). That prefix *anti-* has two meanings: "against" and "instead of." There are in this world teachers of lies who are opposed to Christ, and their method of "seducing" people is to use lies. They offer a substitute Christ, a substitute salvation, and a substitute Bible. They want to give you something instead of the real Word of God and real eternal life.

Christ is the Truth (John 14:6), but Satan is the liar (8:44). The Devil leads people astray—not necessarily with gross sensual sins, but with half-truths and outright lies. He began his career by seducing man in the garden of Eden. He asked Eve, "Yea, hath God said?" Even then, he did not appear to her in his true nature, but masqueraded as a beautiful creature (cf. 2 Cor. 11:13–15).

Satan today often spreads his lies even through religious groups! Not every man standing in a pulpit is preaching the truth of the Word of God. False preachers and false religious teachers have always been among the Devil's favorite and most effective tools.

How can Christians today detect Satan's lies? How can they identify false teachers? How can they grow in their own knowledge of the truth so that they will not be victims of false doctrines?

John answered these questions. The life that is real is characterized by discernment.

The Holy Spirit, referred to by John as "the anointing … ye have received of Him" (1 John 2:27), is Christ's answer to our need for discernment. The Spirit is our Teacher; it is He who enables us to detect truth and error and to remain ("abide") in Christ. He is our protection against ignorance, deception, and untruth.

The discernment of false doctrines and of false teachers will come to our attention again.

**(5) That we may know we are saved (5:13).** We have already touched on this truth, but it is so important that it bears repeating. The life that is real is not built on the empty hopes—or wishes—based on human supposings. It is built on assurance. In fact, as you read John's letter you encounter the word *know* more than thirty times. No Christian, if he is asked whether or not he is going to heaven, needs to say "I hope so," or "I think so." He need have no doubt whatever.

The life that is real is such a free and exciting life because it is based on knowledge of solid facts. "Ye shall know the truth, and the truth shall make you free," promised Jesus (John 8:32). "We have not followed cunningly devised fables" (2 Peter 1:16) was the testimony of Jesus' disciples. These men, almost all of whom died for their faith, did not give their lives for a clever hoax of their own devising, as some critics of Christianity fatuously assert. They knew what they had seen!

Years ago a traveling entertainer billed himself as "The Human Fly." He would climb up the sides of buildings or monuments without the aid of ropes or the protection of nets. Usually the whole neighborhood would turn out to watch him.

During one performance, the Human Fly came to a point on the wall of the building and paused as though he didn't know what to do next. Then he reached with his right arm to take hold of a piece of mortar to lift himself higher. But instead of moving higher, he fell back with a scream and was killed on the pavement below.

When the police opened his right hand, it did not contain a piece of mortar. It contained a handful of dirty cobwebs! The Fly had tried to climb on cobwebs, and it just didn't work.

Jesus warned against such false assurance in the passage that we have already quoted. Many who profess to be Christians will be rejected in the day of God's judgment.

John was saying in his letter, "I want you to be sure that you have eternal life."

As you read this fascinating letter, you will discover that John frequently repeated himself. He wove three themes in and out of these chapters: obedience, love, and truth. In 1 John 1 and 2, the apostle emphasized fellowship, and he told us that the conditions for fellowship are obedience (1 John 1:5—2:6), love (1 John 2:7–17), and truth (1 John 2:18–29).

In the latter half of his letter, John dealt primarily with sonship—our being "born of God." How can a person really know he is a child of God? Well, said John, sonship is revealed by obedience (1 John 3), love (1 John 4), and truth (1 John 5).

Obedience—love—truth. Why did John use these particular tests of fellowship and sonship? For a very practical reason.

When God made us, He made us in His own image (Gen. 1:26–27). This means that we have a personality patterned after God's. We have a mind to think with, a heart to feel with, and a will with which to make decisions. We sometimes refer to these aspects of our personality as intellect, emotion, and will.

The life that is real must involve all the elements of the personality.

Most people are dissatisfied today because their total personality has never been controlled by something real and meaningful. When a person is born of God through faith in Christ, God's Spirit comes into his life to live there forever. As he has fellowship with God in reading and studying the Bible and in prayer, the Holy Spirit is able to control his mind, heart, and will. And what happens then?

A Spirit-controlled mind knows and understands truth.

A Spirit-controlled heart feels love.

A Spirit-controlled will inclines toward obedience.

John wanted to impress this fact on us, and that is why he used a series of contrasts in his letter: truth vs. lies, love vs. hatred, and obedience vs. disobedience.

There is no middle ground in the life that is real. We must be on one side or on the other.

This, then, is the life that is real. It was revealed in Christ; it was experienced by those who trusted in Christ; and it can be shared today.

This life begins with sonship and continues in fellowship. First we are born of God; then we walk (live) with God.

This means that there are two kinds of people who cannot enter into the joy and victory about which we are thinking: those who have never been born of God and those who, though saved, are out of fellowship with God.

It would be a wise thing for us to take inventory spiritually (cf. 2 Cor. 13:5) to see whether or not we qualify to enjoy the spiritual experience with which John's letter deals.

We have already emphasized the importance of being born of God, but if you have any doubts or questions, a review of Fact 2 might be beneficial.

If a true believer is out of fellowship with God, it is usually for one of three reasons:

1. He has disobeyed God's will.

2. He is not getting along with fellow believers.

3. He believes a lie and therefore is living a lie.

Even a Christian can be mistaken in his understanding of truth. That's why John warned us, "Little children, let no man deceive you" (1 John 3:7).

These three reasons parallel John's three important themes: obedience, love, and truth. Once a believer discovers why he is out of fellowship with God, he should confess that sin (or those sins) to the Lord and claim His full forgiveness (1 John 1:9—2:2). A believer can never have joyful fellowship with the Lord if sin stands between them.

God's invitation to us today is "Come and enjoy fellowship with Me and with each other! Come and share the life that is real!"

# QUESTIONS FOR PERSONAL REFLECTION
# OR GROUP DISCUSSION

1. How easy is it for you to believe in things that can't be seen, heard, or sensed in some other physical way? Why is that?

2. According to John, a satisfying reality can be found not in things or thrills, but in a Person. Why is Jesus Christ more real than things or thrills?

3. Why can't the created world alone reveal God's love to us?

4. Why is Jesus called "the Word of Life"?

5. Wiersbe compares a counterfeit Christian to counterfeit money. Why is it important to understand the truth he's trying to get across?

6. Wiersbe lists John's five reasons for sharing his beliefs in this letter. Choose one or two of these and tell why they matter to you.

7. Do you think a Christian can have true fellowship with an unbeliever? Why or why not?

8. "It isn't necessary for Christians to sin." What does that mean? How do you respond?

9. "Most people are dissatisfied today because their total personality has never been controlled by something real and meaningful." Do you agree? Explain.

10. Explain how the Christian life begins with sonship and continues in fellowship.

11. Look at Wiersbe's three reasons why believers usually fall out of fellowship with God. Why are each of these so crucial?

# Chapter Two

# WALKING AND TALKING

## (1 John 1:5—2:6)

E very form of life has its enemies. Insects have to watch out for hungry birds, and birds must keep an eye on hungry cats and dogs. Even human beings have to dodge automobiles and fight off germs.

The life that is real also has an enemy, and we read about it in this section. This enemy is sin. Nine times in these verses John mentioned sin, so the subject is obviously not unimportant. John illustrated his theme by using the contrast between light and darkness: God is light; sin is darkness.

But there is another contrast here too—the contrast between saying and doing. Four times John wrote, "If we say" or "He that saith" (1 John 1:6, 8, 10; 2:4). It is clear that our Christian life is to amount to more than mere "talk"; we must also "walk," or live, what we believe. If we are in fellowship with God (if we are "walking in the light"), our lives will back up what our lips are saying. But if we are living in sin ("walking in darkness"), then our lives will contradict what our lips are saying, making us hypocrites.

The New Testament calls the Christian life a "walk." This walk begins with a step of faith when we trust Christ as our Savior. But salvation is not the end—it's only the beginning—of spiritual life. "Walking" involves progress, and Christians are supposed to advance in the spiritual life. Just as a child must learn to walk and must overcome many difficulties in doing so, a Christian must learn to "walk in the light." And the fundamental difficulty involved here is this matter of sin.

Of course, sin is not simply outward disobedience; sin is also inner rebellion or desire. For example, we are warned about the desires of the flesh and of the eyes and about the pride of life (1 John 2:16), all of which are sinful. Sin is also transgression of the law (3:4), or literally, "lawlessness." Sin is refusal to submit to the law of God. Lawlessness, or independence of the law, is the very essence of sin. If a believer decides to live an independent life, how can he possibly walk in fellowship with God? "Can two walk together except they be agreed?" (Amos 3:3).

Neither in the Old Testament nor in the New does the Bible whitewash the sins of the saints. In escaping a famine, Abraham became weak in his faith and went down to Egypt and lied to Pharaoh (Gen. 12). Later, the patriarch tried to "help God" by marrying Hagar and begetting a son (Gen. 16). In both cases, God forgave Abraham his sin, but Abraham had to reap what he had sowed. God can and will cleanse the record, but He does not change the results. No one can unscramble an egg.

Peter denied the Lord three times and tried to kill a man in the garden when Jesus was arrested. Satan is a liar and a murderer (John 8:44), and Peter was playing right into his hands! Christ forgave Peter (see John 21), of course, but what Peter had done hurt his testimony greatly and hindered the Lord's work.

The fact that Christians sin bothers some people—especially new Christians. They forget that their receiving the new nature does not eliminate the old nature they were born with. The old nature (which has its origin in our physical birth) fights against the new nature, which we receive when we are born again (Gal. 5:16–26). No amount of self-discipline, no set of man-made rules and regulations, can control this old nature. Only the Holy Spirit of God can enable us to "put to death" the old nature (Rom. 8:12–13) and produce the Spirit's fruit (Gal. 5:22–23) in us through the new nature.

Sinning saints are not mentioned in the Bible to discourage us, but to warn us.

"Why do you keep preaching to us Christians about sin?" an angry church member said to her pastor. "After all, sin in the life of a Christian is different from sin in the life of an unsaved person!"

"Yes," replied the pastor, "it is different. It's much worse!"

All of us, therefore, must deal with our sins if we are to enjoy the life that is real. In this section, John explained three approaches to sin.

## 1. WE CAN TRY TO COVER OUR SINS (1:5–6, 8, 10; 2:4)

"God is light, and in him is no darkness at all" (1 John 1:5). When we were saved, God called us out of darkness into His light (1 Peter 2:9). We are children of light (1 Thess. 5:5). Those who do wrong hate light (John 3:19–21). When light shines in on us, it reveals our true nature (Eph. 5:8–13).

Light produces life and growth and beauty, but sin is darkness; and darkness and light cannot exist in the same place. If we are walking in the light, the darkness has to go. If we are holding to sin, then the light goes. There is no middle ground, no vague "gray" area, where sin is concerned.

How do Christians try to cover up their sins? By telling lies! First, we tell lies to others (1 John 1:6). We want our Christian friends to think we are "spiritual," so we lie about our lives and try to make a favorable impression on them. We want them to think that we are walking in the light, though in reality we are walking in the darkness.

Once one begins to lie to others, he will sooner or later lie to himself, and our passage deals with this (1 John 1:8). The problem now is not deceiving others, but deceiving ourselves. It is possible for a believer to live in sin yet convince himself that everything is fine in his relationship to the Lord.

Perhaps the classic example of this is King David (2 Sam. 11—12). First David lusted after Bathsheba. Then he actually committed adultery. Instead of openly admitting what he had done, he tried to cover his sin. He tried to deceive Bathsheba's husband, made him drunk, and had him killed. He lied to himself and tried to carry on his royal duties in the usual way. When his court chaplain, the prophet Nathan, confronted him with a similar hypothetical situation, David condemned the other man, though he felt no condemnation at all for himself. Once we begin to lie to others, it may not be long before we actually believe our lies.

But the spiritual decline becomes still worse: The next step is trying to lie to God (1 John 1:10). We have made ourselves liars; now we try to make God a liar! We contradict His Word, which says that "all have sinned," and we maintain that we are exceptions to the rule. We apply God's Word to others but not to ourselves. We sit through church services or Bible studies and are not touched by the Bible's teachings. Believers who have reached this low level are usually highly critical of other Christians, but they strongly resist applying the Word to their own lives.

The Holy Spirit's inspired picture of the human heart is devastating indeed! A believer lies about his fellowship (1 John 1:6); about his nature— "I could never do a thing like that!" (v. 8); and about his actions (v. 10).

Sin has a deadly way of spreading, doesn't it?

At this point we must discuss an extremely important factor in our experience of the life that is real. That factor is honesty. We must be honest with ourselves, honest with others, and honest with God. Our passage describes a believer who is living a dishonest life: He is a phony. He is playing a role and acting a part, but is not living a genuine life. He is insincere.

What losses does this kind of person experience?

For one thing, he loses the Word. He stops "doing the truth" (1 John 1:6); then the truth is no longer in him (v. 8); and then he turns the truth into lies (v. 10)! "Thy word is truth" (John 17:17), said Jesus, but a person who lives a lie loses the Word. One of the first symptoms of walking in darkness is a loss of blessing from the Bible. You cannot read the Word profitably while you are walking in the dark.

But a dishonest person loses something else: He loses his fellowship with God and with God's people (1 John 1:6–7). As a result, prayer becomes an empty form to him. Worship is dull routine. He becomes critical of other Christians and starts staying away from church: "What communion hath light with darkness?" (2 Cor. 6:14).

A backslidden husband, for example, who is walking in spiritual darkness, out of fellowship with God, can never enjoy full fellowship with his Christian wife, who is walking in the light. In a superficial way, the couple can have companionship; but true spiritual fellowship is impossible. This inability to share spiritual experiences causes many personal problems in homes and between members of local churches.

A group of church members were discussing their new pastor.

"For some reason," said one man, "I really don't feel at ease with him. I believe he's a good man, all right—but something seems to stand between us."

Another member replied, "Yes, I think I know what you mean. I used to have that same problem with him, but now I don't have it anymore. The pastor and I have great fellowship."

"What did he do to make things better?"

"He didn't do anything," said the friend. "I did the changing."

"You did the changing?"

"Yes, I decided to be open and honest about things, the way our pastor is. You see, there isn't one stain of hypocrisy in his life, and there was so much pretending in my life that we just didn't make it together. He and I both knew I was a phony. Since I've started to live an honest Christian life, everything is better."

One problem with dishonesty is that just keeping a record of our lies and pretenses is a full-time job! Abraham Lincoln used to say that if a man is going to be a liar, he had better have a good memory! When a person uses up all his energy in pretending, he has nothing left for living, and life becomes shallow and tasteless. A person who pretends not only robs himself of reality, but he also keeps himself from growing: His true self is smothered under the false self.

The third loss is really the result of the first two: The believer loses his character (1 John 2:4). The process starts out with his telling lies, and it ends up with his becoming a liar! His insincerity, or lack of truthfulness, is at first a role that he plays. Then it is no longer a role—it has become the very essence of his life. His character has eroded. He is no longer a liar because he tells lies; he now tells lies because he is a confirmed liar.

Is it any wonder that God warns, "He that covereth his sins shall not prosper" (Prov. 28:13)? David tried to cover his sins and it cost him his health (Ps. 32:3–4), his joy (Ps. 51), his family, and almost his kingdom. If we want to enjoy the life that is real, we must never cover our sins. What should we do?

## 2. WE CAN CONFESS OUR SINS (1:7, 9)

John gave two interesting titles to Jesus Christ: "advocate" and "propitiation" (1 John 2:1–2). It's important that we understand these two titles because they stand for two ministries that only the Lord Himself performs.

Let's begin with "propitiation." If you look this word up in the dictionary, you may get the wrong idea of its meaning. The dictionary tells us that "to propitiate" means "to appease someone who is angry." If you apply this to Christ, you get the horrible picture of an angry God, about to destroy the world, and a loving Savior giving Himself to appease the irate

God—and this is not the Bible picture of salvation! Certainly God is angry at sin; after all, He is infinitely holy. But the Bible reassures us that "God so loved [not hated] the world" (John 3:16).

No, the word *propitiation* does not mean the appeasing of an angry God. Rather, it means the satisfying of God's holy law. "God is light" (1 John 1:5), and therefore He cannot close His eyes to sin. But "God is love" (4:8) too and wants to save sinners.

How, then, can a holy God uphold His own justice and still forgive sinners? The answer is in the sacrifice of Christ. At the cross, God in His holiness judged sin. God in His love offers Jesus Christ to the world as Savior. God was just in that He punished sin, but He is also loving in that He offers free forgiveness through what Jesus did at Calvary. (Read 1 John 4:10, and also give some thought to Rom. 3:23–26.)

Christ is the Sacrifice for the sins of the whole world, but He is Advocate only for believers. "We [Christians] have an advocate with the Father." The word *advocate* used to be applied to lawyers. The word John used is the very same word Jesus used when He was talking about the coming of the Holy Spirit (John 14:16, 26; 15:26). It means, literally, "one called alongside." When a man was summoned to court, he took an advocate (lawyer) with him to stand at his side and plead his case.

Jesus finished His work on earth (John 17:4)—the work of giving His life as a sacrifice for sin. Today He has an "unfinished work" in heaven. He represents us before God's throne. As our High Priest, He sympathizes with our weaknesses and temptations and gives us grace (Heb. 4:15–16; 7:23–28). As our Advocate, He helps us when we sin. When we confess our sins to God, because of Christ's advocacy, God forgives us.

The Old Testament contains a beautiful picture of this. Joshua was the Jewish high priest after the Jews returned to their land following their captivity in Babylon (Zech. 3:1–7). (Don't confuse this Joshua with the Joshua who conquered the Promised Land.) The nation had sinned; to symbolize this, Joshua stood before God in filthy garments and Satan stood at Joshua's right hand to accuse him (cf. Rev. 12:10). God the Father was the Judge; Joshua, representing the people, was the accused; Satan was the prosecuting attorney. (The Bible calls him the accuser of the brethren.) It looked as if Satan had an open-and-shut case. But Joshua had an Advocate who stood at God's right hand, and this changed the situation. Christ gave Joshua a change of garments and silenced the accusations of Satan.

This is what is in view when Jesus Christ is called our "advocate." He represents believers before God's throne, and the merits of His sacrifice make possible the forgiveness of the believer's sin. Because Christ died for His people, He satisfied the justice of God. ("The wages of sin is death.") Because He lives for us at God's right hand, He can apply His sacrifice to our needs day by day.

All He asks is that when we have failed, we confess our sins.

What does it mean to "confess"? Well, to confess sins means much more than simply to "admit" them. The word confess actually means "to say the same thing [about]." To confess sin, then, means to say the same thing about it that God says about it.

A counselor was trying to help a man who had come forward during an evangelistic meeting. "I'm a Christian," the man said, "but there's sin in my life, and I need help." The counselor showed him 1 John 1:9 and suggested that the man confess his sins to God.

"O Father," the man began, "if we have done anything wrong—"

"Just a minute!" the counselor interrupted. "Don't drag me into your sin! My brother, it's not 'if' or 'we'—you'd better get down to business with God!"

The counselor was right.

Confession is not praying a lovely prayer, or making pious excuses, or trying to impress God and other Christians. True confession is naming sin—calling it by name what God calls it: envy, hatred, lust, deceit, or whatever it may be. Confession simply means being honest with ourselves and with God, and if others are involved, being honest with them too. It is more than admitting sin. It means judging sin and facing it squarely.

When we confess our sins, God promises to forgive us (1 John 1:9). But this promise is not a "magic rabbit's foot" that makes it easy for us to disobey God!

"I went out and sinned," a student told his campus chaplain, "because I knew I could come back and ask God to forgive me."

"On what basis can God forgive you?" the chaplain asked, pointing to 1 John 1:9.

"God is faithful and just," the boy replied.

"Those two words should have kept you out of sin," the chaplain said. "Do you know what it cost God to forgive your sins?"

The boy hung his head. "Jesus had to die for me."

Then the chaplain zeroed in. "That's right—forgiveness isn't some cheap sideshow trick God performs. God is faithful to His promise, and God is just, because Christ died for your sins and paid the penalty for you. Now, the next time you plan to sin, remember that you are going to sin against a faithful, loving God!"

Of course, cleansing has two sides to it: the judicial and the personal. The blood of Jesus Christ, shed on the cross, delivers us from the guilt of sin and gives us right standing ("justification") before God. God is able to forgive because Jesus' death has satisfied His holy law.

But God is also interested in cleansing a sinner inwardly. David prayed, "Create in me a clean heart, O God" (Ps. 51:10). When our confession is sincere, God does a cleansing work (1 John 1:9) in our hearts by His Spirit and through His Word (John 15:3).

The great mistake King David made was in trying to cover his sins instead of confessing them. For perhaps a whole year he lived in deceit and defeat. No wonder he wrote that a man should pray "in a time of finding out" (Ps. 32:6, literal translation).

When should we confess our sins? Immediately when we discover it! "He that covereth his sins shall not prosper; but whoso confesseth and forsaketh them shall have mercy" (Prov. 28:13). By walking in the light, we are able to see the "dirt" in our lives and deal with it immediately.

This leads to a third way to deal with sins.

## 3. WE CAN CONQUER OUR SINS (2:1–3, 5–6)

John makes it clear that Christians do not have to sin. "I am writing these things to you that you may not sin" (1 John 2:1 NASB).

The secret of victory over sin is found in the phrase "walk in the light" (1 John 1:7).

To walk in the light means to be open and honest, to be sincere. Paul prayed that his friends might "be sincere and without offense" (Phil. 1:10). The word *sincere* comes from two Latin words, *sine* and *cera*, which mean "without wax." It seems that in Roman days, some sculptors covered up their mistakes by filling the defects in their marble statues with wax, which was not readily visible—until the statue had been exposed to the hot sun awhile. But more dependable sculptors made certain that their customers knew that the statues they sold were *sine cera*—without wax.

It is unfortunate that churches and Bible classes have been invaded by insincere people, people whose lives cannot stand to be tested by God's light. "God is light," and when we walk in the light, there is nothing we can hide. It is refreshing to meet a Christian who is open and sincere and is not trying to masquerade!

To walk in the light means to be honest with God, with ourselves, and with others. It means that when the light reveals our sins to us, we immediately confess them to God and claim His forgiveness. And if our sins injure another person, we ask his or her forgiveness too.

But walking in the light means something else: It means obeying God's Word (1 John 2:3–4). "Thy word is a lamp unto my feet and a light unto my path" (Ps. 119:105). To walk in the light means to spend time daily in God's Word, discovering His will; and then obeying what He has told us.

Obedience to God's Word is proof of our love for Him. There are three motives for obedience. We can obey because we have to, because we need to, or because we want to.

A slave obeys because he has to. If he doesn't obey he will be punished. An employee obeys because he needs to. He may not enjoy his work, but he does enjoy getting his paycheck! He needs to obey because he has a family to feed and clothe. But a Christian is to obey his heavenly Father because he wants to—for the relationship between him and God is one of love. "If you love me, keep my commandments" (John 14:15).

This is the way we learned obedience when we were children. First, we obeyed because we had to. If we didn't obey, we were spanked! But as we grew up, we discovered that obedience meant enjoyment and reward; so we started obeying because it met certain needs in our lives. And it was a mark of real maturity when we started obeying because of love.

"Baby Christians" must constantly be warned or rewarded. Mature Christians listen to God's Word and obey it simply because they love Him.

Walking in the light involves honesty, obedience, and love; it also involves following the example of Christ and walking as He walked (1 John 2:6). Of course, nobody ever becomes a Christian by following Christ's example, but after we come into God's family, we are to look to Jesus Christ as the one great example of the kind of life we should live.

This means "abiding in Christ." Christ is not only the Propitiation (or sacrifice) for our sins (1 John 2:2) and the Advocate who represents us before God (2:1), but He is also the perfect Pattern (He is "Jesus Christ the righteous") for our daily lives.

The key statement here is "as he is." "Because as he is, so are we in this world" (1 John 4:17). We are to walk in the light "as he is in the light" (1:7). We are to purify ourselves "even as he is pure" (3:3). "He that doeth righteousness is righteous, even as He is righteous" (v. 7). Walking in the light means living here on earth the way Jesus lived when He was here and the way He is right now in heaven.

This has extremely practical applications in our daily lives. For example, what should a believer do when another believer sins against him? The answer is that believers should forgive one another "even as God for Christ's sake hath forgiven you" (Eph. 4:32; cf. Col. 3:13).

Walking in the light—following the example of Christ—will affect a home. Husbands are supposed to love their wives "even as Christ also loved the church" (Eph. 5:25). Husbands are supposed to care for their wives "even as the Lord" cares for the church (v. 29). And wives are to honor and obey their husbands (vv. 22–24).

No matter what area of life it may be, our responsibility is to do what Jesus would do. "As he is, so are we in this world." We should "walk [live] even as He walked [lived]."

Jesus Himself taught His disciples what it means to abide in Him. He explained it in His illustration of the vine and its branches (John 15). Just as the branch gets its life by remaining in contact with the vine, so believers receive their strength by maintaining fellowship with Christ.

To abide in Christ means to depend completely on Him for all that we need in order to live for Him and serve Him. It is a living relationship. As He lives out His life through us, we are able to follow His example and walk as He walked. Paul expressed this experience perfectly: "Christ liveth in me" (Gal. 2:20).

This is a reference to the work of the Holy Spirit. Christ is our Advocate in heaven (1 John 2:1), to represent us before God when we sin. The Holy Spirit is God's Advocate for us here on earth. Christ is making intercession for us (Rom. 8:34), and the Holy Spirit is also making intercession for us (vv. 26–27). We are part of a fantastic "heavenly party line": God the Son prays for us in heaven, and God the Spirit prays for us in our hearts. We have fellowship with the Father through the Son, and the Father has fellowship with us through the Spirit.

Christ lives out His life through us by the power of the Spirit, who lives within our bodies. It is not by means of imitation that we abide in Christ and walk as He walked. No, it is through incarnation: Through His Spirit, "Christ liveth in me." To walk in the light is to walk in the Spirit and not fulfill the lusts of the flesh (see Gal. 5:16).

God has made provisions for us in these ways to conquer sin. We can never lose or change the sin nature that we were born with (1 John 1:8), but we need not obey its desires. As we walk in the light and see sin as it actually is, we will hate it and turn from it. And if we sin, we immediately confess it to God and claim His cleansing. By depending on the power of the indwelling Spirit, we abide in Christ and "walk as He walked."

But all this begins with openness and honesty before God and men. The minute we start to act a part, to pretend, to impress others, we step out of the light and into shadows. Sir Walter Scott put it this way:

Oh, what a tangled web we weave

When first we practice to deceive!

The life that is real cannot be built on things that are deceptive. Before we can walk in the light, we must know ourselves, accept ourselves, and yield ourselves to God. It is foolish to try to deceive others, because God already knows what we really are!

All this helps to explain why walking in the light makes life so much easier and happier. When you walk in the light, you live to please only one Person—God. This really simplifies things! Jesus said, "I do always those things that please him" (John 8:29). We "ought to walk and to please God" (1 Thess. 4:1). If we live to please ourselves and God, we are trying to serve two masters, and this never works. If we live to please men, we will always be in trouble because no two men will agree and we will find ourselves caught in the middle. Walking in the light—living to please God—simplifies our goals, unifies our lives, and gives us a sense of peace and poise.

John made it clear that the life that is real has no love for sin. Instead of trying to cover sin, a true believer confesses sin and tries to conquer it by walking in the light of God's Word. He is not content simply to know he is going to heaven. He wants to enjoy that heavenly life right here and now. "As He is, so are we in this world." He is careful to match his walk and his talk. He does not try to impress himself, God, or other Christians with a lot of "pious talk."

A congregation was singing as a closing hymn the familiar song "For You I Am Praying." The speaker turned to a man on the platform and asked quietly, "For whom are you praying?"

The man was stunned. "Why, I guess I'm not praying for anybody. Why do you ask?"

"Well, I just heard you say, 'For you I am praying,' and I thought you meant it," the preacher replied. "Oh, no," said the man. "I'm just singing."

Pious talk! A religion of words! To paraphrase James 1:22, "We should be doers of the Word as well as talkers of the Word." We must walk what we talk. It is not enough to know the language; we must also live the life. "If we say—" then we ought also to do!

# QUESTIONS FOR PERSONAL REFLECTION OR GROUP DISCUSSION

1. How can Christians benefit from the Bible's teaching about "sinning saints"?

2. Do you agree that sin in the life of a Christian is worse than sin in the life of an unbeliever? Why or why not?

3. How do Christians try to cover up their sins?

4. Why is honesty with ourselves, others, and God so important in the Christian life?

5. How can we build into our lives the habit of honesty with ourselves, others, and God about our sins?

6. How is Jesus our Advocate?

7. Wiersbe thinks it's essential to name our sins as God would when we are confessing them. Do you agree or disagree? Why?

8. How does our motivation for obedience change as we mature?

9. What does it mean to "walk in the light"? Give a practical example.

10. "Before we can walk in the light, we must know ourselves, accept ourselves, and yield ourselves to God." Do you agree? Explain.

# Chapter Three

# SOMETHING OLD, SOMETHING NEW

## (1 John 2:7–11)

I just *love* that hat!"

"Man, I really *love* the old-fashioned kind of baked beans!"

"But, Mom, don't you realize that Tom and I *love* each other?"

Words, like coins, can be in circulation for such a long time that they start wearing out. Unfortunately, the word *love* is losing its value and is being used to cover a multitude of sins.

It is really difficult to understand how a man can use the same word to express his love for his wife as he uses to tell how he feels about baked beans! When words are used that carelessly, they really mean little or nothing at all. Like the dollar, they have been devalued.

As John described the life that is real, he used three words repeatedly: life, love, and light. In fact, he devoted three sections of his letter to the subject of Christian love. He explained that *love*, *life*, and *light* belong together. Read these three sections (1 John 2:7–11; 3:10–24; 4:7–21) without the intervening verses, and you will see that love, life, and light must not be separated.

In our present study (1 John 2:7–11), we learn how Christian love is affected by light and darkness. A Christian who is walking in the light (which simply means he is obeying God) is going to love his brother Christian.

In 1 John 3:10–24, we are told that Christian love is a matter of life or death: To live in hatred is to live in spiritual death. In 1 John 4:7–21 we see that Christian love is a matter of truth or error (cf. v. 6): Because we know God's love toward us, we show God's love toward others.

In these three sections, then, we find three good reasons why Christians should love one another:

1. God has commanded us to love (1 John 2:7–11).

2. We have been born of God and God's love lives in us (1 John 3:10–24).

3. God first revealed His love to us (1 John 4:7–21). "We love … because He first loved us" (v. 19).

John not only wrote about love but also practiced it. One of his favorite names for his readers was "Beloved." He felt love for them. John is known as the "apostle of love" because in his gospel and his epistles he gives such prominence to this subject. However, John was not always the apostle of love. At one time Jesus gave John and his brother James, both of whom had hot tempers, the nickname "Boanerges" (Mark 3:17), which means "sons of thunder." On another occasion these two brothers wanted to call down fire from heaven to destroy a village (Luke 9:51–56).

Since the New Testament was written in Greek, the writers were often able to use more precise language. It is unfortunate that our English word *love* has so many shades of meaning (some of them contradictory). When we read in 1 John about "love," the Greek word used is *agape* (ah-GAH-pay), the word for God's love toward man, a Christian's love for other Christians, and God's love for His church (Eph. 5:22–33).

Another Greek word for love, *philia* (fee-LEE-ah), used elsewhere, carries the idea of "friendship love," which is not quite as profound or divine as agape love. (The Greek word for sensual love, *eros*, from which we get our word *erotic*, is not used at all in the New Testament.)

The amazing thing is that Christian love is both old and new (1 John 2:7–8). This seems to be a contradiction. Love itself, of course, is not new, nor is the commandment—that men love God and one another—a new thing. Jesus Himself combined two Old Testament commandments, Deuteronomy 6:5 and Leviticus 19:18, and said (Mark 12:28–34) that these two commandments summarize all the law and the prophets. Loving God and loving one's neighbor were old, familiar responsibilities before Jesus ever came to earth.

In what sense, then, is "love one another" a "new" commandment (1 John 2:8)? Again, a look at the Greek helps to answer the question.

The Greeks had two different words for "new." One means "new in time," and the other means "new in quality." For example, you would use the first word to describe the latest car, a recent model. But if you purchased a car that was so revolutionary that it was radically different, you would use the second word—new in quality. (Our English words *recent* and *fresh* just about make this distinction: *Recent* means "new in time," *fresh* means "new in character.")

The commandment to love one another is not new in time, but it is new in character. Because of Jesus Christ, the old commandment to "love one another" has taken on new meaning. We learn in these five brief verses (1 John 2:7–11) that the commandment is new in three important ways.

## 1. IT IS NEW IN EMPHASIS (2:7)

In the previous paragraph (1 John 2:3–6), John had been talking about "the commandments" in general, but now he narrowed his focus down to one single commandment. In the Old Testament, the command that God's people love one another was only one of many, but now this old commandment is lifted out and given a place of preeminence.

How is it possible for one commandment to stand head and shoulders above all the others? This is explained by the fact that love is the fulfillment of God's law (Rom. 13:8–10).

Parents must care for their children according to law. Child neglect is a serious crime. But how many parents have a conversation like this when the alarm clock goes off in the morning?

She: "Honey, you'd better get up and go to work. We don't want to get arrested."

He: "Yeah, and you'd better get up and get breakfast for the kids, and get their clothes ready. The cops might show up and put us both in jail."

She: "You're right. Boy, it's a good thing they have a law, or we'd stay in bed all day!"

It's doubtful that the fear of the law is often the motive behind earning a living or caring for one's children. Parents fulfill their responsibilities (even if grudgingly on occasion) because they love each other and their children. To them, doing the right thing is not a matter of law—it's a matter of love.

The commandment "Love one another" is the fulfillment of God's law in the same way. When you love people, you do not lie about them or steal from them. You have no desire to kill them. Love for God and love for others motivates a person to obey God's commandments without even thinking about them! When a person acts out of Christian love he obeys God and serves others—not because of fear, but because of his love.

This is why John said that "Love one another" is a new commandment—it is new in emphasis. It is not simply one of many commandments. No, it stands at the top of the list!

But it is new in emphasis in another way too. It stands at the very beginning of the Christian life. "The old commandment is the word which ye had from the beginning" (1 John 2:7). This phrase "from the beginning" is used in two different ways in John's letter, and it is important that you distinguish them. In 1 John 1:1, describing the eternality of Christ, we read that He existed "from the beginning." In John 1:1—a parallel verse—we read, "In the beginning was the Word."

But in 1 John 2:7, the subject is the beginning of the Christian life. The commandment to love one another is not an appendix to our Christian experience, as though God had an afterthought. No! It is in our hearts from the very beginning of our faith in Jesus Christ. If this were not so, John could not have written, "We know that we have passed out of death into life because we love the brethren" (1 John 3:14 NASB). And Jesus said, "By this all men will know that you are My disciples, if you have love for one another" (John 13:35 NASB).

By nature, an unsaved person may be selfish and even hateful. As much as we love a newborn baby, we must confess that the infant is self-centered and thinks the whole world revolves around his crib. The child is typical of an unsaved person. "We ourselves also were sometimes foolish, disobedient, deceived, serving divers lusts and pleasures, living in malice and envy, hateful and hating one another" (Titus 3:3). This unretouched photo of the unbeliever may not be beautiful, but it is certainly accurate! Some unregenerate persons do not display the traits here mentioned, but the works of the flesh (Gal. 5:19–21) are always potentially present in their dispositions.

When a sinner trusts Christ, he receives a new life and a new nature. The Holy Spirit of God comes to live in him, and the love of God is "shed abroad in [his] heart" by the Spirit (Rom. 5:5). God does not have to give a new believer a long lecture about love! "For ye yourselves are taught of God [i.e., by the Holy Spirit within you] to love one another" (1 Thess. 4:9). A new believer discovers that he now hates what he used to love, and that he loves what he used to hate!

So the commandment to love one another is new in emphasis: It is one of the most important commandments Christ gave us (John 13:34).

In fact, "love one another" is repeated at least a dozen times in the New Testament (John 13:34; 15:9, 12, 17; Rom. 13:8; 1 Thess. 4:9; 1 Peter 1:22; 1 John 3:11, 23; 4:7, 11–12; 2 John 5). And there are many other references to brotherly love.

It is important that we understand the meaning of Christian love. It is not a shallow sentimental emotion that Christians try to "work up" so they can get along with one another. It is a matter of the will rather than an emotion—an affection for and attraction to certain persons. It is a matter of determining—of making up your mind—that you will allow God's love to reach others through you, and then of acting toward them in loving ways. You are not to act "as if you loved them," but because you love them. This is not hypocrisy—it is obedience to God.

Perhaps the best explanation of Christian love is 1 Corinthians 13. You should read a modern translation of this chapter to get the full force of its message: The Christian life without love is *nothing!*

But the commandment "Love one another" is not only new in emphasis. It is new in another way.

## 2. It Is New in Example (2:8)

"Love one another," John pointed out, was first true in Christ, and now it is true in the lives of those who are trusting Christ. Jesus Himself is the greatest example of this commandment.

Later on we will think about that great statement "God is love" (1 John 4:8), but it is anticipated here. When one looks at Jesus Christ, one sees love embodied and exemplified. In commanding us to love, Jesus does not ask us to do something that He has not already done Himself. The four gospel records are the account of a life lived in the spirit of love—and that life was lived under conditions far from ideal. Jesus says to us, in effect, "I lived by this great commandment, and I can enable you to follow My example."

Jesus illustrated love by the very life that He lived. He never showed hatred or malice. His righteous soul hated all sin and disobedience, but He never hated the people who committed such sins. Even in His righteous announcements of judgment, there was always an undercurrent of love.

It is encouraging to think of Jesus' love for the twelve disciples. How they must have broken His heart again and again as they argued over who was the greatest or tried to keep people from seeing their Master. Each of them was different from the others, and Christ's love was broad enough to include each one in a personal, understanding way. He was patient with Peter's impulsiveness, Thomas's unbelief, and even Judas's treachery. When Jesus commanded His disciples to love one another, He was only telling them to do as He had done.

Consider too our Lord's love for all kinds of people. The publicans and sinners were attracted by His love (Luke 15:1), and even the lowest of the low could weep at His feet (Luke 7:36–39). Spiritually hungry Rabbi Nicodemus could meet with Him privately at night (John 3:1–21), and four thousand of the "common people" could listen to His teaching for three days (Mark 8:1–9) and then receive a miraculous meal from Him. He held babies in His arms. He spoke about children at play. He even comforted the women who wept as the soldiers led Him out to Calvary.

Perhaps the greatest thing about Jesus' love was the way it touched even the lives of His enemies. He looked with loving pity on the religious leaders who in their spiritual blindness accused Him of being in league with Satan (Matt. 12:24). When the mob came to arrest Him, He could have called on the armies of heaven for protection, but He yielded to His enemies. And then He died for them—for His enemies! "Greater love hath no man than this, that a man lay down his life for his friends" (John 15:13). But Jesus died not only for His friends, but also for His foes! And as they crucified Him, He prayed for them: "Father, forgive them, for they know not what they do."

In His life, in His teachings, and in His death, Jesus is the perfect example of this new commandment, "Love one another." And this is what helps to make the commandment "new." In Christ we have a new illustration of the old truth that God is love and that the life of love is the life of joy and victory.

What is true in Christ ought to be true in each believer. "As he is, so are we in this world" (1 John 4:17). A believer should live a life of Christian love "because the darkness is passing away, and the true Light is already shining" (1 John 2:8 NASB). This reminds us of the emphasis on walking in the light (1 John 1). Two ways of life are contrasted: Those who walk in the light practice love; those who walk in the darkness practice hatred. The Bible repeatedly emphasizes this truth.

"The darkness is passing away," but the light does not yet shine fully all over the world, nor does it penetrate every area of even a believer's life.

When Christ was born, "the dayspring from on high" visited the world (Luke 1:78). "Dayspring" means sunrise. The birth of Christ was the beginning of a new day for mankind! As He lived before men, taught them, and ministered to them, He spread the light of life and love. "The people which sat in darkness saw great light; and to them which sat in the region and shadow of death light is sprung up" (Matt. 4:16).

But there is a conflict in this world between the forces of light and the forces of darkness. "And the light is shining in the darkness, and the darkness is not able to put it out" (John 1:5, literal translation). Satan is the Prince of Darkness, and he extends his evil kingdom by means of lies and hatred. Christ is the "Sun of righteousness" (Mal. 4:2), and He extends His kingdom by means of truth and love.

The kingdoms of Christ and of Satan are in conflict today, but "the path of the just is as the shining light, that shineth more and more unto the perfect day" (Prov. 4:18). The darkness is passing away little by little, and the True Light is shining brighter and brighter in our hearts.

Jesus Christ is the standard of love for Christians. "A new commandment I give unto you, that ye love one another," He said, "as I have loved you, that ye also love one another" (John 13:34). And He repeated: "This is my commandment, that ye love one another, as I have loved you" (John 15:12). We are not to measure our Christian love against the love of some other Christian (and we usually pick somebody whose life is more of an excuse than an example!) but against the love of Jesus Christ our Lord. The old commandment becomes "new" to us as we see it fulfilled in Christ.

So the commandment "Love one another" is new in emphasis and new in example. It is also new in a third way.

### 3. IT IS NEW IN EXPERIENCE (2:9–11)

Our passage continues the illustration of light and darkness. If a Christian walks in the light and is in fellowship with God, he will also be in fellowship with others in God's family. Love and light go together, much as hatred and darkness go together.

It is easy to talk about Christian love, but much more difficult to practice it. For one thing, such love is not mere talk (1 John 2:9). For a Christian to say (or sing!) that he loves the brethren while he actually hates another believer is for him to lie. In other words (and this is a sobering truth), it is impossible to be in fellowship with the Father and out of fellowship with another Christian at the same time.

This is one reason why God established the local church, the fellowship of believers. "You can't be a Christian alone"; a person cannot live a complete and developing Christian life unless he is in fellowship with God's people. The Christian life has two relationships: the vertical (Godward) and the horizontal (manward). And what God has joined together, man must not put asunder! And each of these two relationships is to be one of love one for the other.

Jesus dealt with this matter in the Sermon on the Mount (see Matt.

5:21–26). A gift on the altar was valueless as long as the worshipper had a dispute to settle with his brother. Note that Jesus did not say that the worshipper had something against his brother, but that the brother had something against the worshipper. But even when we have been offended, we should not wait for the one who has offended us to come to us; we should go to him. If we do not, Jesus warned us that we will end up in a prison of spiritual judgment where we will have to pay the last penny (Matt. 18:21–35). In other words, when we harbor an unforgiving, unloving spirit, we harm ourselves most.

The contrast between "saying" and "doing" is one we have met before (1 John 1:6, 8, 10; 2:4, 6). It is easy to practice a Christianity of "words"—singing the right songs, using the right vocabulary, praying the right prayers—and through it all, deceiving ourselves into thinking we are spiritual. This mistake also ties into something Jesus taught in the Sermon on the Mount (Matt. 5:33–37). What we say should be the true expression of our character. We should not need extra words ("oaths") to fortify what we say. Our yes should mean yes, and our no should mean no. So, if we say we are in the light, we will prove it by loving the brethren. Many Christians urgently need to be accepted, loved, and encouraged.

Contrary to popular opinion, Christian love is not "blind." When we practice true Christian love, we find life getting brighter and brighter. Hatred is what darkens life! When true Christian love flows out of our hearts, we will have greater understanding and perception in spiritual things. This is why Paul prayed that our love may grow in knowledge and perception, that we may distinguish the things that differ (see Phil. 1:9–10). A Christian who loves his brother is a Christian who sees more clearly.

No book in the Bible illustrates the blinding power of hatred like the book of Esther. The events recorded there take place in Persia, where many of the Jews were living after the captivity. Haman, one of the king's chief men, had a burning hatred for the Jews. The only way he could satisfy this hatred was to see the whole nation destroyed. He plunged ahead in an evil plot, completely blind to the fact that the Jews would win and that he himself would be destroyed.

Hatred is blinding people today too. Christian love is not a shallow sentiment, a passing emotion that we perhaps experience in a church service. Christian love is a practical thing; it applies in the everyday affairs of life. Just consider the "one another" statements in the New Testament and you will see how practical it is to love one another. Here are just a few (there are over twenty such statements):

Wash one another's feet (John 13:14).

Prefer one another (Rom. 12:10).

Be of the same mind one to another (Rom. 12:16).

Do not judge one another (Rom. 14:13).

Receive one another (Rom. 15:7).

Admonish one another (Rom. 15:14).

Edify [build up] one another (1 Thess. 5:11).

Bear one another's burdens (Gal. 6:2).

Confess your faults to one another (James 5:16).

Use hospitality one to another (1 Peter 4:9).

In short, to love other Christians means to treat them the way God treats them—and the way God treats us. Christian love that does not show itself in action and in attitude is spurious (see 1 Cor. 13:4–7).

What happens to a believer who does not love the brethren? We have already seen the first tragic result: He lives in the darkness, though he probably thinks he is living in the light (1 John 2:9). He thinks he sees, but he is actually blinded by the darkness of hatred. This is the kind of person who causes trouble in Christian groups. He thinks he is a "spiritual giant," with great understanding, when actually he is a babe with very little spiritual perception. He may read the Bible faithfully and pray fervently, but if he has hatred in his heart, he is living a lie.

The second tragic result is that such a believer becomes a cause of stumbling (see 1 John 2:10). It is bad enough when an unloving believer hurts himself (1 John 2:9), but when he starts to hurt others, the situation is far more serious. It is serious to walk in the darkness. It is dangerous to walk in the darkness when stumbling blocks are in the way! An unloving brother stumbles himself, and in addition he causes others to stumble.

A man who was walking down a dark street one night saw a pinpoint of light coming toward him in a faltering way. He thought perhaps the person carrying the light was ill or drunk, but as he drew nearer he could see a man with a flashlight carrying a white cane.

"Why would a blind man be carrying a light?" the man wondered, and then he decided to ask.

The blind man smiled. "I carry my light, not so I can see, but so that others can see me. I cannot help being blind," he said, "but I can help being a stumbling block."

The best way to help other Christians not to stumble is to love them. Love makes us stepping-stones; hatred (or any of its "cousins," such as envy or malice) makes us stumbling blocks. It is important that Christians exercise love in a local church, or else there will always be problems and disunity. When we are falling over each other, instead of lifting each other higher, we will never become a truly happy spiritual family.

Apply this, for instance, to the delicate matter of "questionable things" (Rom. 14—15). Since believers come from different backgrounds, they do not always agree. In Paul's day, they differed on such matters as diets and holy days. One group said it was unspiritual to eat meat offered to idols. Another group wanted strict observance of the Sabbath. There were several facets to the problem, but basic to its solution was "Love one another!" Paul put it this way: "Let us not, therefore, judge one another anymore; but judge this, rather, that no man put a stumbling block or an occasion to fall in his brother's way.… But if thy brother be grieved with thy food, now walkest thou not in love" (Rom. 14:13, 15 sco).

A third tragic result of hatred is that it retards a believer's spiritual progress (1 John 2:11). A blind man—a person who is walking in darkness—can never find his way! The only atmosphere that is conducive to spiritual growth is the atmosphere of spiritual light—of love. Just as the fruits and flowers need sunshine, so God's people need love if they are going to grow.

The commandment "Love one another" becomes new to us in our own day-by-day experiences. It is not enough for us to recognize that it is new in emphasis and say, "Yes, love is important!" Nor is it enough for us to see God's love exemplified by Jesus Christ. We must know this love in our own experience. The old commandment "Love one another" becomes a new commandment as we practice God's love in daily life.

Thus far, we have seen the negative side of 1 John 2:9–11; now let's look at the positive. If we practice Christian love, what will the wonderful results be?

First of all, we will be living in the light—living in fellowship with God and with our Christian brothers.

Second, we will not stumble or become stumbling blocks to others.

And third, we will grow spiritually and will progress toward Christlikeness.

At this point, we should think about the contrast between the ugly "works of the flesh" (Gal. 5:19–21) and the beautiful fruit of the Spirit— "Love, joy, peace, patience, gentleness, goodness, faith, meekness, and self-control" (Gal. 5:22–23). When we are walking in the light, the "seed of the Word" (Luke 8:11) can take root and bear fruit. And the first cluster the Spirit produces is love!

But love does not live alone. Love produces joy! Hatred makes a man miserable, but love always brings him joy.

A Christian couple came to see a pastor because their marriage was beginning to fall apart. "We're both saved," the discouraged husband said, "but we just aren't happy together. There's no joy in our home." As the pastor talked with them and they considered together what the Bible has to say, one fact became clear: Both the husband and wife were nursing grudges. Each recalled many annoying little things the other had done!

"If you two really loved each other," said the pastor, "you wouldn't file these hurts away in your hearts. Grudges fester in our hearts like infected sores and poison the whole system."

Then he read, "[Love] thinketh no evil" (1 Cor. 13:5). He explained, "This means that love never keeps records of things others do that hurt us. When we truly love someone, our love covers their sins and helps to heal the wounds they cause." Then he read, "And above all things have fervent love among yourselves; for love shall cover the multitude of sins" (1 Peter 4:8 SCO).

Before the couple left, the pastor counseled them: "Instead of keeping records of the things that hurt, start remembering the things that please. An unforgiving spirit always breeds poison, but a loving spirit that sees and remembers the best always produces health."

A Christian who walks in love is always experiencing some new joy because the "fruit of the Spirit" is love and joy. And when we blend "love" and "joy," we will have "peace"—and peace helps to produce "patience." In other words, walking in the light, walking in love, is the secret of Christian growth, which nearly always begins with love.

Now, all of us must admit that we cannot generate Christian love under our own power. By nature, we are selfish and hateful. It is only as God's Spirit floods our hearts with love that we, in turn, can love one another. "The love of God is shed abroad in our hearts by the Holy Ghost which is given unto us" (Rom. 5:5). The Spirit of God makes the commandment "Love one another" into a new and exciting day-by-day experience. If we walk in the light, God's Spirit produces love. If we walk in darkness, our own selfish spirit produces hatred.

The Christian life—the life that is real—is a beautiful blending of "something old, something new." The Holy Spirit takes the "old things" and makes them "new things" in our experience. When you stop to think about it, the Holy Spirit never grows old! He is always young! And He is the only Person on earth today who was here centuries ago when Jesus lived, taught, died, and rose again. He is the only One who can take "old truth" and make it fresh and new in our daily experience at this present time.

There are other exciting truths in the rest of John's letter, but if we fail to obey in this matter of love, the rest of the letter may well be "darkness" to us. Perhaps the best thing we can do, right now, is to search our hearts to see if we hold anything against a brother, or if someone has anything against us. The life that is real is an honest life—and it is a life of doing, not merely saying. It is a life of active love in Christ. This means forgiveness, kindness, long-suffering. But it also means joy and peace and victory.

The love life is the only life, because it is the life that is real!

# QUESTIONS FOR PERSONAL REFLECTION
# OR GROUP DISCUSSION

1. Wiersbe lists three basic reasons for Christians to love one another. Which of these motivate you personally? Are there any of them that, in all honesty, you have to admit don't yet motivate you?

2. What are the three Greek words for love, and how do they differ? Why does this matter?

3. How is loving one another a "new commandment" through Jesus Christ?

4. "Love for God and love for others motivates a person to obey God's commandments without even thinking about them." Do you agree? Why?

5. What is your definition of true Christian love?

6. What were some practical ways Jesus demonstrated His love while on earth?

7. "It is impossible to be in fellowship with the Father and out of fellowship with another Christian at the same time." Do you agree? Explain.

8. What are some of the practical ways the New Testament tells us to love one another?

9. How does loving a fellow Christian help prevent him or her from stumbling?

10. How can Christians develop more Christian love?

# Chapter Four

# THE LOVE GOD HATES
## (1 John 2:12–17)

group of first graders had just completed a tour of a hospital, and the nurse who had directed them was asking for questions. Immediately a hand went up.

"How come the people who work here are always washing their hands?" a little fellow asked.

After the laughter had subsided, the nurse gave a wise answer: "They are 'always washing their hands' for two reasons. First, they love health; and second, they hate germs."

In more than one area of life, love and hate go hand in hand. A husband who loves his wife is certainly going to exercise a hatred for what would harm her. "Ye that love the LORD, hate evil" (Ps. 97:10). "Let love be without hypocrisy. Abhor what is evil; cling to what is good" (Rom. 12:9 NASB).

John's epistle has reminded us to exercise love (1 John 2:7–11)—the right kind of love. Now it warns us that there is a wrong kind of love, a love that God hates. This is love for what the Bible calls "the world."

There are four reasons why Christians should not love "the world."

## 1. BECAUSE OF WHAT THE WORLD IS

The New Testament word *world* has at least three different meanings. It sometimes means the physical world, the earth: "God that made the world [our planet] and all things therein" (Acts 17:24). It also means the human world, mankind: "For God so loved the world" (John 3:16). Sometimes these two ideas appear together: "He [Jesus] was in the world, and the world [earth] was made by him, and the world [mankind] knew him not" (1:10).

But the warning "Love not the world!" is not about the world of nature or the world of men. Christians ought to appreciate the beauty and usefulness of the earth God has made, since He "giveth us richly all things to enjoy" (1 Tim. 6:17). And they certainly ought to love people—not only their friends, but even their enemies.

This "world" named here as our enemy is an invisible spiritual system opposed to God and Christ.

We use the word *world* in the sense of system in our daily conversation. The TV announcer says, "We bring you the news from the world of sports." "The world of sports" is not a separate planet or continent. It is an organized system made up of a set of ideas, people, activities, purposes, and so forth. And "the world of finance" and "the world of politics" are likewise systems of their own. Behind what we see in sports or finance is an invisible system that we cannot see, and it is the system that "keeps things going."

"The world," in the Bible, is Satan's system for opposing the work of Christ on earth. It is the very opposite of what is godly and holy and spiritual (1 John 2:16). "We know that we are of God, and the whole world lies in the power of the evil one" (5:19 NASB). Jesus called Satan "the prince of this world" (John 12:31). The Devil has an organization of evil spirits (Eph. 6:11–12) working with him and influencing the affairs of "this world."

Just as the Holy Spirit uses people to accomplish God's will on earth, so Satan uses people to fulfill his evil purposes. Unsaved people, whether they realize it or not, are energized by "the prince of the power of the air, the spirit that now worketh in the children of disobedience" (Eph. 2:1–2).

Unsaved people belong to "this world." Jesus called them "the children of this world" (Luke 16:8). When Jesus was here on earth, the people of "this world" did not understand Him, nor do they now understand those of us who trust Him (1 John 3:1). A Christian is a member of the human world, and he lives in the physical world, but he does not belong to the spiritual world that is Satan's system for opposing God. "If ye were of the world [Satan's system], the world would love his own; but because ye are not of the world, but I have chosen you out of the world, therefore the world hateth you" (John 15:19).

"The world," then, is not a natural habitat for a believer. The believer's citizenship is in heaven (Phil. 3:20 NASB), and all his effective resources for living on earth come from his Father in heaven.

The believer is somewhat like a scuba diver. The water is not man's natural habitat, for he is not equipped for life in (or under) it. When a scuba diver goes under, he has to take special equipment with him so that he can breathe.

Were it not for the Holy Spirit's living within us, and the spiritual resources we have in prayer, Christian fellowship, and the Word, we could never "make it" here on earth. We complain about the pollution of earth's atmosphere—the atmosphere of "the world" is also so polluted spiritually that Christians cannot breathe normally!

But there is a second—and more serious—reason why Christians must not love the world.

## 2. BECAUSE OF WHAT THE WORLD DOES TO US (2:15–16)

"If any man love the world, the love of the Father is not in him" (1 John 2:15).

Worldliness is not so much a matter of activity as of attitude. It is possible for a Christian to stay away from questionable amusements and doubtful places and still love the world, for worldliness is a matter of the heart. To the extent that a Christian loves the world system and the things in it, he does not love the Father.

Worldliness not only affects your response to the love of God; it also affects your response to the will of God. "The world passeth away ... but he that doeth the will of God abideth forever" (1 John 2:17).

Doing the will of God is a joy for those living in the love of God. "If ye love me, keep my commandments." But when a believer loses his enjoyment of the Father's love, he finds it hard to obey the Father's will.

When you put these two factors together, you have a practical definition of worldliness: Anything in a Christian's life that causes him to lose his enjoyment of the Father's love or his desire to do the Father's will is worldly and must be avoided. Responding to the Father's love (your personal devotional life), and doing the Father's will (your daily conduct)—these are two tests of worldliness.

Many things in this world are definitely wrong, and God's Word identifies them as sins. It is wrong to steal and to lie (Eph. 4:25, 28). Sexual sins are wrong (5:1–3). About these and many other actions, Christians can have little or no debate. But there are areas of Christian conduct that are not so clear and about which even the best Christians disagree. In such cases, each believer must apply the test to his own life and be scrupulously honest in his self-examination, remembering that even a good thing may rob a believer of his enjoyment of God's love and his desire to do God's will.

A senior student in a Christian college was known for his excellent grades and his effective Christian service. He was out preaching each weekend, and God was using him to win the souls and challenge Christians.

Then something happened: His testimony was no longer effective, his grades began to drop, and even his personality seemed to change. The president called him in.

"There's been a change in your life and your work," the president said, "and I wish you'd tell me what's wrong."

The student was evasive for a time, but then he told the story. He was engaged to a lovely Christian girl and was planning to get married after graduation. He had been called to a fine church and was anxious to move his new bride into the parsonage and get started in the pastorate.

"I've been so excited about it that I've even come to the place where I don't want the Lord to come back!" he confessed. "And then the power dropped out of my life."

His plans—good and beautiful as they were—came between him and the Father. He lost his enjoyment of the Father's love. He was worldly!

John pointed out that the world system uses three devices to trap Christians: "the lust [desire] of the flesh, the lust of the eyes, and the pride of life" (1 John 2:16). These same devices trapped Eve back in the garden: "And when the woman saw that the tree was good for food [the lust of the flesh], and that it was pleasant to the eyes [the lust of the eyes], and a tree to be desired to make one wise [the pride of life], she took of the fruit" (Gen. 3:6).

The lust of the flesh includes anything that appeals to man's fallen nature. "The flesh" does not mean "the body." Rather, it refers to the basic nature of unregenerate man that makes him blind to spiritual truth (1 Cor. 2:14). Flesh is the nature we receive in our physical birth; spirit is the nature we receive in the second birth (John 3:5–6). When we trust Christ, we become "partakers of the divine nature" (2 Peter 1:4). A Christian has both the old nature (flesh) and the new nature (Spirit) in his life. And what a battle these two natures can wage (Gal. 5:17–23)!

God has given man certain desires, and these desires are good. Hunger, thirst, weariness, and sex are not at all evil in themselves. There is nothing wrong about eating, drinking, sleeping, or begetting children. But when the flesh nature controls them, they become sinful "lusts." Hunger is not evil, but gluttony is sinful. Thirst is not evil, but drunkenness is a sin. Sleep is a gift of God, but laziness is shameful. Sex is God's precious gift when used rightly; but when used wrongly, it becomes immorality.

Now you can see how the world operates. It appeals to the normal appetites and tempts us to satisfy them in forbidden ways. In today's world we are surrounded by all kinds of allurements that appeal to our lower nature—and "the flesh is weak" (Matt. 26:41). If a Christian yields to it, he will get involved in the "works of the flesh." (Gal. 5:19–21 gives us the ugly list.)

It is important that a believer remember what God says about his old nature, the flesh. Everything God says about the flesh is negative. In the flesh there is "no good thing" (Rom. 7:18). The flesh profits "nothing" (John 6:63). A Christian is to put "no confidence" in the flesh (Phil. 3:3). He is to make "no provision" for the flesh (Rom. 13:14 NASB). A person who lives for the flesh is living a negative life.

The second device that the world uses to trap the Christian is called "the lust of the eyes." We sometimes forget that the eyes can have an appetite! (Have you ever said, "Feast your eyes on this"?)

The lust of the flesh appeals to the lower appetites of the old nature, tempting us to indulge them in sinful ways. The lust of the eyes, however, operates in a more refined way. In view here are pleasures that gratify the sight and the mind—sophisticated and intellectual pleasures. Back in the days of the apostle John, the Greeks and Romans lived for entertainments and activities that excited the eyes. Times have not changed very much! In view of television, perhaps every Christian's prayer ought to be "Turn away my eyes from looking at vanity" (Ps. 119:37 NASB).

Achan (Josh. 7), a soldier, brought defeat to Joshua's army because of the lust of his eyes. God had warned Israel not to take any spoils from the condemned city of Jericho, but Achan did not obey. He explained: "When I saw among the spoils a goodly Babylonish garment, and two hundred shekels of silver, … then I coveted them, and took them" (Josh. 7:21). The lust of the eyes led him into sin, and his sin led the army into defeat.

The eyes (like the other senses) are a gateway into the mind. The lust of the eyes, therefore, can include intellectual pursuits that are contrary to God's Word. There is pressure to make Christians think the way the world thinks. God warns us against "the counsel of the ungodly." This does not mean that Christians ignore education and secular learning; it does mean they are careful not to let intellectualism crowd God into the background.

The third device is the "boastful pride of life" (1 John 2:16 NASB). God's glory is rich and full; man's glory is vain and empty. In fact, the Greek word for "pride" was used to describe a braggart who was trying to impress people with his importance. People have always tried to outdo others in their spending and their getting. The boastful pride of life motivates much of what such people do.

Why is it that so many folks buy houses, cars, appliances, or wardrobes that they really cannot afford? Why do they succumb to the "travel now, pay later" advertising and get themselves into hopeless debt taking vacations far beyond their means? Largely because they want to impress other people—because of their "pride of life." They may want folks to notice how affluent or successful they are.

Most of us do not go that far, but it is amazing what stupid things people do just to make an impression. They even sacrifice honesty and integrity in return for notoriety and a feeling of importance.

Yes, the world appeals to a Christian through the lust of the flesh, the lust of the eyes, and the pride of life. And once the world takes over in one of these areas, a Christian will soon realize it. He will lose his enjoyment of the Father's love and his desire to do the Father's will. The Bible will become boring and prayer a difficult chore. Even Christian fellowship may seem empty and disappointing. It is not that there is something wrong with others, however—what's wrong is the Christian's worldly heart.

It is important to note that no Christian becomes worldly all of a sudden. Worldliness creeps up on a believer; it is a gradual process. First is the friendship of the world (James 4:4). By nature, the world and the Christian are enemies. ("Marvel not, my brethren, if the world hate you," 1 John 3:13.) A Christian who is a friend of the world is an enemy of God.

Next, the Christian becomes spotted by the world (James 1:27). The world leaves its dirty marks on one or two areas of his life. This means that gradually the believer accepts and adopts the ways of the world.

When this happens, the world ceases to hate the Christian and starts to love him! So John warned us, "Love not the world!"—but too often our friendship with the world leads to love. As a result, the believer becomes conformed to the world (Rom. 12:2), and you can hardly tell the two apart.

Among Christians, worldliness rears its ugly head in many subtle and unrecognized forms. Sometimes we tend to idolize great athletes, TV stars, or political leaders who profess to be Christians—as if these individuals were able to be of special help to Almighty God. Or we cater to wealthy and "influential" persons in our local church, as if God's work would fold up without their good will or financial backing. Many forms of worldliness do not involve reading the wrong books and indulging in "carnal" amusements.

Sad to say, being conformed to the world can lead a Christian into being "condemned with the world" (1 Cor. 11:32). If a believer confesses and judges this sin, God will forgive him, but if he does not confess, God must lovingly chasten him. When a Christian is "condemned with the world," he does not lose his sonship. Rather, he loses his testimony and his spiritual usefulness. And in extreme cases, Christians have even lost their lives (see vv. 29–30)!

The downward steps and their consequences are illustrated in the life of Lot (Gen. 13:5–13; 14:8–14; 19). First Lot looked toward Sodom. Then he pitched his tent toward Sodom in the well-watered plains of Jordan. Then he moved into Sodom. And when Sodom was captured by the enemy, Lot was captured too. He was a believer (2 Peter 2:6–8), but he had to suffer with the unbelieving sinners of that wicked city. And when God destroyed

Sodom, everything Lot lived for went up in smoke! Lot was saved so as by fire and lost his eternal reward (1 Cor. 3:12–15).

No wonder John warned us not to love the world!

## 3. BECAUSE OF WHAT A CHRISTIAN IS (2:12–14)

This raises a practical and important question about the nature of a Christian and how he keeps from getting worldly.

The answer is found in the unusual form of address used in 1 John 2:12–14. Note the titles used as John addressed his Christian readers: "little children ... fathers ... young men ... little children."

What was he referring to?

To begin with, "little children" (1 John 2:12) refers to all believers. Literally, this word means "born ones." All Christians have been born into God's family through faith in Jesus Christ, and their sins have been forgiven. The very fact that one is in God's family, sharing His nature, ought to discourage one from becoming friendly with the world. To be friendly with the world is treachery! "Friendship of the world is enmity with God ... whosoever therefore will be [wants to be] a friend of the world is the enemy of God" (James 4:4).

But something else is true: We begin as little children—born ones— but we must not stay that way! Only as a Christian grows spiritually does he overcome the world.

John mentioned three kinds of Christians in a local church family: fathers, young men, and little children (1 John 2:12–14). The "fathers," of course, are mature believers who have an intimate personal knowledge of God. Because they know God, they know the dangers of the world. No Christian who has experienced the joys and wonders of fellowship with God, and of service for God, will want to live on the substitute pleasures this world offers.

The "young men" are the conquerors: They have overcome the wicked one, Satan, who is the prince of this world system. How did they overcome him? Through the Word of God! "I have written unto you, young men, because ye are strong, and the Word of God abideth in you" (1 John 2:14). The "young men," then, are not yet fully mature, but they are maturing, for they use the Word of God effectively. The Word is the only weapon that will defeat Satan (Eph. 6:17).

The "little children" addressed in 1 John 2:13 are not those addressed in 1 John 2:12; two different Greek words are used. The word in 1 John 2:13 carries the idea of "immature ones," or little children still under the authority of teachers and tutors. These are young Christians who have not yet grown up in Christ. Like physical children, these spiritual children know their father, but they still have some growing to do.

Here, then, is the Christian family! All of them are "born ones," but some of them have grown out of infancy into spiritual manhood and adulthood. It is the growing, maturing Christian to whom the world does not appeal. He is too interested in loving his Father and in doing his Father's will. The attractions of the world have no allure for him. He realizes that the things of the world are only toys, and he can say with Paul, "When I became a man, I put away childish things" (1 Cor. 13:11).

A Christian stays away from the world because of what the world is (a satanic system that hates and opposes Christ), because of what the world does to us (attracts us to live on sinful substitutes), and because of what he (the Christian) is—a child of God.

## 4. Because of Where the World Is Going (2:17)

"The world is passing away!" (see 1 John 2:17).

That statement would be challenged by many men today who are confident that the world—the system in which we live—is as permanent as anything can be. But the world is not permanent. The only sure thing about this world system is that it is not going to be here forever. One day the system will be gone, and the pleasant attractions within it will be gone: All are passing away. What is going to last?

Only what is part of the will of God!

Spiritual Christians keep themselves "loosely attached" to this world because they live for something far better. They are "strangers and pilgrims on the earth" (Heb. 11:13). "For here have we no continuing city, but we seek one to come" (13:14). In Bible times, many believers lived in tents because God did not want them to settle down and feel at home in this world.

John was contrasting two ways of life: a life lived for eternity and a life lived for time. A worldly person lives for the pleasures of the flesh, but a dedicated Christian lives for the joys of the Spirit. A worldly believer lives for what he can see, the lust of the eyes, but a spiritual believer lives for the unseen realities of God (2 Cor. 4:8–18). A worldly minded person lives for the pride of life, the vainglory that appeals to men, but a Christian who does the will of God lives for God's approval. And he "abideth forever."

Every great nation in history has become decadent and has finally been conquered by another nation. There is no reason why we should suppose that our nation will be an exception. Some nineteen world civilizations in the past have slipped into oblivion. There is no reason why we should think that our present civilization will endure forever. "Change and decay in all around I see," wrote Henry F. Lyte (1793–1847), and if our civilization is not eroded by change and decay it will certainly be swept away and replaced by a new order of things at the coming of Christ, which could happen at any time.

Slowly but inevitably, and perhaps sooner than even Christians think, the world is passing away, but the man who does God's will abides forever.

This does not mean that all God's servants will be remembered by future generations. Of the multitudes of famous men who have lived on earth, less than two thousand have been remembered by any number of people for more than a century.

Nor does it mean that God's servants will live on in their writings or in the lives of those they influenced. Such "immortality" may be a fact, but it is equally true of unbelievers such as Karl Marx, Voltaire, or Adolf Hitler.

No, we are told here (1 John 2:17) that Christians who dedicate themselves to doing God's will—to obeying God—"abide [remain] forever." Long after this world system—with its vaunted culture, its proud philosophies, its egocentric intellectualism, and its godless materialism—has been forgotten, and long after this planet has been replaced by the new heavens and the new earth, God's faithful servants will remain—sharing the glory of God for all eternity.

And this prospect is not limited to Moody, Spurgeon, Luther, or Wesley and their likes—it is open to each and every humble believer. If you are trusting Christ, it is for you.

This present world system is not a lasting one. "The fashion of this world passeth away" (1 Cor. 7:31). Everything around us is changing, but the things that are eternal never change. A Christian who loves the world will never have peace or security because he has linked his life with that which is in a state of flux. "He is no fool," wrote missionary martyr Jim Elliot, "who gives what he cannot keep to gain what he cannot lose."

The New Testament has quite a bit to say about "the will of God." One of the "fringe benefits" of salvation is the privilege of knowing God's will (Acts 22:14). In fact, God wants us to be "filled with the knowledge of his will" (Col. 1:9). The will of God is not something that we consult occasionally like an encyclopedia. It is something that completely controls our lives. The issue for a dedicated Christian is not simply "Is it right or wrong?" or "Is it good or bad?" The key issue is "Is this the will of God for me?"

God wants us to understand His will (Eph. 5:17), not just know what it is. "He made known his ways unto Moses, his acts unto the children of Israel" (Ps. 103:7). Israel knew what God was doing, but Moses knew why He was doing it! It is important that we understand God's will for our lives and see the purposes He is fulfilling.

After we know the will of God, we should do it from the heart (Eph. 6:6). It is not by talking about the Lord's will that we please Him, but by doing what He tells us (Matt. 7:21). And the more we obey God, the better able we are to discover and follow God's will (Rom. 12:2). Discovering and doing God's will is something like learning to swim: You must get into the water before it becomes real to you. The more we obey God, the more proficient we become in knowing what He wants us to do.

God's goal for us is that we will "stand ... complete in all the will of God" (Col. 4:12). This means to be mature in God's will.

A little child constantly asks his parents what is right and what is wrong and what they want him to do or not to do. But as he lives with his parents and experiences their training and discipline, he gradually discovers what their will for him is. In fact, a disciplined child can "read his father's mind" just by watching the parent's face and eyes! An immature Christian is always asking his friends what they think God's will is for him. A mature Christian stands complete in the will of God. He knows what the Lord wants him to do.

How does one discover the will of God? The process begins with surrender: "Present your bodies a living sacrifice ... be not conformed to this world ... that ye may prove [know by experience] what is that good, and acceptable, and perfect, will of God" (Rom. 12:1–2). A Christian who loves the world will never know the will of God in this way. The Father shares His secrets with those who obey Him. "If any man will do his will, he shall know of the doctrine" (John 7:17). And God's will is not a "spiritual cafeteria" where a Christian takes what he wants and rejects the rest! No, the will of God must be accepted in its entirety. This involves a personal surrender to God of one's entire life.

God reveals His will to us through His Word. "Thy word is a lamp unto my feet, and a light unto my path" (Ps. 119:105). A worldly believer has no appetite for the Bible. When he reads it, he gets little or nothing from it. But a spiritual believer, who spends time daily reading the Bible and meditating on it, finds God's will there and applies it to his everyday life.

We may also learn God's will through circumstances. God moves in wonderful ways to open and close doors. We must test this kind of leading by the Word of God—and not test the Bible's clear teaching by circumstances!

Finally, God leads us into His will through prayer and the working of His Spirit in our hearts. As we pray about a decision, the Spirit speaks to us. An "inner voice" may agree with the leading of circumstances. We are never to follow this "inner voice" alone: We must always test it by the Bible, for it is possible for the flesh (or for Satan) to use circumstances—or "feelings"—to lead us completely astray.

To sum it up, a Christian is in the world physically (John 17:11), but he is not of the world spiritually (v. 14). Christ has sent us into the world to bear witness of Him (v. 18). Like a scuba diver, we must live in an alien element, and if we are not careful, the alien element will stifle us. A Christian cannot help being in the world, but when the world is in the Christian, trouble starts!

The world gets into a Christian through his heart: "Love not the world!" Anything that robs a Christian of his enjoyment of the Father's love, or of his desire to do the Father's will, is worldly and must be avoided. Every believer, on the basis of God's Word, must identify those things for himself.

A Christian must decide, "Will I live for the present only, or will I live for the will of God and abide forever?" Jesus illustrated this choice by telling about two men. One built on the sand and the other on the rock (Matt. 7:24–27). Paul referred to the same choice by describing two kinds of material for building: temporary and permanent (1 Cor. 3:11–15).

Love for the world is the love God hates. It is the love a Christian must shun at all costs!

# QUESTIONS FOR PERSONAL REFLECTION
## OR GROUP DISCUSSION

1. What are some characteristics of "the world" as John uses the term?

2. Why does God hate the love of the world?

3. What is your definition of worldliness?

4. What is the "lust of the flesh"? Give examples.

5. What is the "lust of the eyes"? Give examples.

6. What is the "pride of life"? Give examples.

7. What are some ways in which you are tempted to worldliness?

8. How does God's Word help us defeat Satan's efforts to lure us into worldliness?

9. Why does godliness require more than avoiding evil and doing good?


10. What does staying only loosely attached to the world involve for you, in practical terms?

# Chapter Five

# TRUTH OR CONSEQUENCES

## (1 John 2:18–29)

I t makes no difference what you believe, just as long as you are sincere!"

That statement expresses the personal philosophy of many people today, but it is doubtful whether most of those who make it have really thought it through. Is "sincerity" the magic ingredient that makes something true? If so, then you ought to be able to apply it to any area of life, and not only to religion.

A nurse in a city hospital gives some medicine to a patient, and the patient becomes violently ill. The nurse is sincere but the medicine is wrong, and the patient almost dies.

A man hears noises in the house one night and decides a burglar is at work. He gets his gun and shoots the "burglar," who turns out to be his daughter! Unable to sleep, she has gotten up for a bite to eat. She ends up the victim of her father's "sincerity."

It takes more than "sincerity" to make something true. Faith in a lie will always cause serious consequences; faith in the truth is never misplaced. It does make a difference what a man believes! If a man wants to drive from Chicago to New York, no amount of sincerity will get him there if the highway is taking him to Los Angeles. A person who is real builds his life on truth, not superstition or lies. It is impossible to live a real life by believing lies.

God has warned the church family ("little children") about the conflict between light and darkness (1 John 1:1—2:6) and between love and hatred (2:7–17). Now He warns them about a third conflict: the conflict between truth and error. It is not enough for a believer to walk in the light and to walk in love; he must also walk in truth. The issue is truth—or consequences!

Before John explained the tragic consequences of turning from the truth, he emphasized the seriousness of the matter. He did so by using two special terms: "the last time" and "antichrist." Both terms make it clear that Christians are living in an hour of crisis and must guard against the errors of the enemy.

"The last time" (or "the last hour") is a term that reminds us that a new age has dawned on the world. "The darkness is past, and the true light now shineth" (1 John 2:8). Since the death and resurrection of Jesus Christ, God is doing a "new thing" in this world. All of Old Testament history prepared the way for the work of Christ on the cross. All history since that time is merely preparation for "the end," when Jesus will come and establish His kingdom. There is nothing more that God must do for the salvation of sinners.

You may ask, "But if it was 'the last hour' in John's day, why has Jesus not yet returned?"

This is an excellent question, and Scripture gives us the answer. God is not limited by time the way His creatures are. God works in human time, but He is above time (see 2 Peter 3:8).

"The last hour" began back in John's day and has been growing in intensity ever since. There were ungodly false teachers in John's day, and during the intervening centuries they have increased both in number and in influence. "The last hour" or "the last times" are phrases that describe a kind of time, not a duration of time. "The latter times" are described in 1 Timothy 4. Paul, like John, observed characteristics of his time, and we see the same characteristics today in even greater intensity.

In other words, Christians have always been living in "the last time"— in crisis days. It is therefore important that you know what you believe and why you believe it.

The second term, "antichrist," is used in the Bible only by John (1 John 2:18, 22; 4:3; 2 John 7). It describes three things: (1) a spirit in the world that opposes or denies Christ; (2) the false teachers who embody this spirit; and (3) a person who will head up the final world rebellion against Christ.

The "spirit of antichrist" (1 John 4:3) has been in the world since Satan declared war on God (see Gen. 3). The "spirit of antichrist" is behind every false doctrine and every "religious" substitute for the realities Christians have in Christ. As I mentioned in chapter 1 of this study, that prefix *anti*- actually has a dual meaning. It can mean, in the Greek, both "against" Christ and "instead of" Christ. Satan in his frenzy is fighting Christ and His eternal truth, and he is substituting his counterfeits for the realities found only in our Lord Jesus.

The "spirit of antichrist" is in the world today. It will eventually lead to the appearance of a "satanic superman," whom the Bible calls "Antichrist" (capital A). He is called "the man of sin" (or "lawlessness") (2 Thess. 2:1–12).

This passage explains that there are two forces at work in today's world: Truth is working through the church by the Holy Spirit, and evil is working by the energy of Satan. The Holy Spirit, in Christians, is holding back lawlessness; but when the church is removed at the rapture (1 Thess. 4:13–18), Satan will be able to complete his temporary victory and take over the world. (John had more to say about this world ruler and his evil system in the book of Revelation, particularly 13:1–18; 16:13; and 19:20.)

Does it make any difference what you believe? It makes all the difference in the world! You are living in crisis days—in the last hour—and the spirit of antichrist is working in the world! It is vitally important that you know and believe the truth and be able to detect lies when they come your way.

John's epistle gives three outstanding marks of the false teacher who is controlled by the "spirit of antichrist."

## 1. He Departs from the Fellowship (2:18–19)

"They went out from us, but they were not really of us; for if they had been of us, they would have remained with us" (1 John 2:19 NASB).

The word *us* refers, of course, to the fellowship of believers, the church. Not everyone who is part of an assembly of believers is necessarily a member of the family of God!

The New Testament presents the church in a twofold way: as one worldwide family and as local units or assemblies of believers. There is a "universal" as well as "local" aspect of the church. The whole worldwide company of believers is compared with a body (1 Cor. 12) and with a building (Eph. 2:19–22). When a sinner trusts Christ as Savior, he receives eternal life and immediately becomes a member of God's family and a part of Christ's spiritual body. He should then identify himself with a local group of Christians (a church) and start serving Christ (Acts 2:41–42). But the point here is that a person can belong to a local church and not be part of the true spiritual body of Christ.

One of the evidences of true Christian life is a desire to be with the people of God. "We know that we have passed from death unto life, because we love the brethren" (1 John 3:14). When people share the same divine nature (2 Peter 1:4) and are indwelt by the same Holy Spirit (Rom. 8:14–16), they want to enjoy fellowship and to share with one another. As we have seen, fellowship means "to have in common." When people have spiritual realities in common, they want to be together.

But the "counterfeit Christians" mentioned in 1 John 2 did not remain in the fellowship. They went out. This doesn't imply that "staying in the church" keeps a person saved; rather, it indicates that remaining in the fellowship is one evidence that a person is truly a Christian. In His parable of the sower (Matt. 13:1–9, 18–23), Jesus makes it clear that only those who produce fruit are truly born again. It is possible to be close to an experience of salvation, and even to have some characteristics that would pass for "Christian," and yet not be a child of God. The people in view in 1 John 2 left the fellowship because they did not possess the true life and the love of Christ was not in their hearts.

There are many unfortunate divisions among the people of God today, but all true Christians have things in common, regardless of church affiliation. They believe that the Bible is the Word of God and that Jesus is the Son of God. They confess that men are sinners and that the only way one can be saved is through faith in Christ. They believe that Christ died as man's substitute on the cross, and that He arose again from the dead. They believe that the Holy Spirit indwells true believers. Finally, they believe that one day in the future Jesus will come again. Christians may differ on other matters—church government, for example, or modes of baptism—but they agree on the basic doctrines of the faith.

If you will investigate the history of the false cults and anti-Christian religious systems in today's world, you will find that in most cases their founders started out in a local church! They were "with us" but not "of us," so they went out "from us" and started their own groups.

Any group, no matter how "religious," that for doctrinal reasons separates itself from a local church that holds to the Word of God, must immediately be suspect. Often these groups follow human leaders and the books men have written, rather than Jesus Christ and God's Word. The New Testament (e.g., 2 Tim. 3—4; 2 Peter 2) makes it clear that it is dangerous to depart from the fellowship.

## 2. HE DENIES THE FAITH (2:20–25; 4:1–6)

The key questions for a Christian are Who is Jesus Christ? Is Christ merely "an example," "a good Man," or "a wonderful teacher"; or is He God come in the flesh?

John's readers knew the truth about Christ, or else they would not have been saved. You all know the truth, because you have the Spirit of God, an unction, and the Spirit teaches you all things (see 1 John 2:20, 27). "Now if any man have not the Spirit of Christ, he is none of his" (Rom. 8:9).

False Christians in John's day used two special words to describe their experience: *knowledge* and *unction*. They claimed to have a special unction (anointing) from God that gave them a unique knowledge. They were "illuminated" and therefore living on a much higher level than anybody else. But John pointed out that all true Christians know God and have received the Spirit of God! And because they have believed the truth, they recognize a lie when they meet it.

The great assertion of the faith that sets a Christian apart from others is this: Jesus Christ is God come in the flesh (1 John 4:2).

Not all preachers and teachers who claim to be Christian are really Christian in their belief (1 John 4:1–6). If they confess that Jesus Christ is God come in the flesh, then they belong to the true faith. If they deny Christ, then they belong to antichrist. They are in and of the world, and are not, like true believers, called out of the world. When they speak, the world (unsaved persons) hears them and believes them. But the unsaved world can never understand a true Christian. A Christian speaks under the direction of the Spirit of Truth; a false teacher speaks under the influence of the spirit of error—the spirit of antichrist.

To confess that "Jesus Christ is God come in the flesh" involves much more than simply to identify Christ. The demons did this (Mark 1:24), but it did not save them. True confession involves personal faith in Christ—in who He is and what He has done. A confession is not a mere intellectual "theological statement" that you recite; it is a personal witness from your heart of what Christ has done for you. If you have trusted Christ and have confessed your faith, you have eternal life (1 John 2:25). Those who cannot honestly make this confession do not have eternal life, which is an ultimately serious matter.

George Whitefield, a great British evangelist, was speaking to a man about his soul. He asked the man, "Sir, what do you believe?"

"I believe what my church believes," the man replied respectfully.

"And what does your church believe?"

"The same thing I believe."

"And what do both of you believe?" the preacher inquired again.

"We both believe the same thing!" was the only reply he could get.

A man is not saved by assenting to a church creed. He is saved by trusting Jesus Christ and bearing witness to his faith (Rom. 10:9–10).

False teachers will often say, "We worship the Father. We believe in God the Father, even though we disagree with you about Jesus Christ."

But to deny the Son means to deny the Father also. You cannot separate the Father and the Son, since both are one God. Jesus said, "I and my Father are one" (John 10:30). He also made it clear that true believers honor both the Father and the Son: "That all men should honor the Son, even as they honor the Father. He that honoreth not the Son honoreth not the Father which hath sent him" (5:23). If you say you "worship one God" but leave Jesus Christ out of your worship, you are not worshipping as a true Christian.

It is important that you stay with the truth of God's Word. The Word (or message) Christians have "heard from the beginning" is all you need to keep you true to the faith. The Christian life continues just as it began: through faith in the Bible's message. A religious leader who comes along with "something new," something that contradicts what Christians have "heard from the beginning," is not to be trusted. "Try the spirits, whether they are of God" (1 John 4:1). Let the Word abide in you (2:24), and abide in Christ (2:28); otherwise you will be led astray by the spirit of antichrist. No matter what false teachers may promise, you have the sure promise of eternal life (v. 25). You need nothing more!

If false teachers were content to enjoy themselves in their own meetings, it would be bad enough; the tragedy is that they try earnestly to convert others to their anti-Christian doctrines. This is the third mark of a man who has turned away from God's truth.

## 3. HE TRIES TO DECEIVE THE FAITHFUL (2:26–29)

It is interesting to observe that anti-Christian groups rarely try to lead lost sinners to their false faith. Instead, they spend much of their time trying to convert professing Christians (and church members, at that) to their own doctrines. They are out to "seduce" the faithful.

The word *seduce* carries the idea of "being led astray." We have been warned that this would happen: "Now the Spirit speaketh expressly, that in the latter times some shall depart from the faith, giving heed to seducing spirits, and doctrines of devils [teachings of demons]" (1 Tim. 4:1).

Jesus called Satan the "father of lies" (John 8:44 NIV). The Devil's purpose is to lead Christians astray by teaching them false doctrines (2 Cor. 11:1–4, 13–15). We should not accept everything a person tells us simply because he claims to believe the Bible, for it is possible to "twist" the Bible to make it mean almost anything (2 Cor. 4:1–2).

Satan is not an originator; he is a counterfeiter. He imitates the work of God. For example, Satan has counterfeit "ministers" (2 Cor. 11:13–15) who preach a counterfeit gospel (Gal. 1:6–12) that produces counterfeit Christians (John 8:43–44) who depend on a counterfeit righteousness (Rom. 10:1–10). In the parable of the tares (Matt. 13:24–30, 36–43), Jesus and Satan are pictured as sowers. Jesus sows the true seed, the children of God, but Satan sows "the children of the wicked one." The two kinds of plants, while growing, look so much alike that the servants could not tell the difference until the fruit appeared! Satan's chief stratagem during this age is to plant the counterfeit wherever Christ plants the true. And it is important that you be able to detect the counterfeit and separate the teachings of Christ from the false teachings of antichrist.

How does a believer do this? By depending on the teaching of the Holy Spirit. Each believer has experienced the anointing (the "unction," 1 John 2:20) of the Spirit, and it is the Spirit who teaches him truth (John 14:17; 15:26). False teachers are not led by the Spirit of Truth; they are led by the spirit of error (1 John 4:3, 6).

The word *anoint* reminds us of the Old Testament practice of pouring oil on the head of a person being set apart for special service. A priest was anointed (Ex. 28:41), and so was a king (1 Sam. 15:1) or a prophet (1 Kings 19:16). A New Testament Christian is anointed, not with literal oil, but by the Spirit of God—an anointing that sets him apart for his ministry as one of God's priests (1 Peter 2:5, 9). It is not necessary for you to pray for "an anointing of the Spirit"; if you are a Christian, you have already received this special anointing. This anointing "abides in us" and therefore does not need to be imparted to us.

We have seen that false teachers deny the Father and the Son; they also deny the Spirit. The Spirit is the Teacher God has given us (John 14:26), but these false Christians want to be teachers themselves and lead others astray. They try to take the place of the Holy Spirit!

We are warned against letting any man be our teacher, for God has given us the Spirit to teach us His truth. This does not deny the office of human teachers in the church (Eph. 4:11–12), but it means that under the guidance of the Spirit you must test the teaching of men as you search the Bible for yourself (see Acts 17:11).

A missionary to the Native Americans was in Los Angeles with a Native American friend who was a new Christian. As they walked down the street, they passed a man on the corner who was preaching with a Bible in his hand. The missionary knew the man represented a cult, but the Native American saw only the Bible. He stopped to listen to the sermon.

"I hope my friend doesn't get confused," the missionary thought, and he began to pray. In a few minutes the Native American turned away from the meeting and joined his missionary friend.

"What did you think of the preacher?" the missionary asked.

"All the time he was talking," exclaimed the Native American, "something in my heart kept saying, 'Liar! Liar!'"

That "something" in his heart was "Someone"—the Holy Spirit of God! The Spirit guides us into the truth and helps us to recognize error. This anointing of God is "no lie," because "the Spirit is truth" (1 John 5:6).

Why are some Christians led astray to believe false teachings? Because they are not abiding in the Spirit. The word *abide* occurs several times in this section of 1 John, and it would be helpful to review:

- False teachers do not abide ("continue") in the fellowship (1 John 2:19).
- The word (message) we have heard should abide in us (1 John 2:24).
- The anointing (the Holy Spirit) abides in us, and we should abide in the Spirit (1 John 2:27).
- As we abide in the Word and in the Spirit, we also abide in Christ (1 John 2:28).
- We noticed this word *abide* earlier in John's letter too:
- If we say we abide in Christ, we should walk as He walked (1 John 2:6).
- If we love our brother, we abide in the light (1 John 2:10).
- If the Word abides in us, we will be spiritually strong (1 John 2:14).
- If we do the will of God, we shall abide forever (1 John 2:17).

"To abide" means to remain in fellowship; and "fellowship" is the key idea in the first two chapters of this epistle. From chapters 3 to 5, the emphasis is on sonship, or being "born of God."

It is possible to be a child in a family and yet be out of fellowship with one's father and with other members of the family. When our heavenly Father discovers that we are out of fellowship with Him, He deals with us to bring us back into the place of abiding. This process is called "chastening"—child training (Heb. 12:5–11).

A believer must allow the Spirit of God to teach him from the Bible. One of the major functions of a local church is the teaching of God's Word (2 Tim. 2:2; 4:1–5). The Spirit gives the gift of teaching to certain individuals in the fellowship (Rom. 12:6–7) and they teach others, but what they teach must be tested (1 John 4:1–3).

There is a difference between deliberate deception and spiritual ignorance. When Apollos preached in the synagogue at Ephesus, his message was correct as far as it went, but it was not complete. Priscilla and Aquila, two mature believers in the congregation, took him aside privately and instructed him in the full message of Christ (Acts 18:24–28). A Christian who spends time daily in the Bible and in prayer will walk in the Spirit and have the discernment he needs.

The Spirit teaches us "of all things" (1 John 2:27). False teachers have a way of "riding a hobby"—prophecy or sanctification or even diet—and neglecting the whole message of the Bible. Jesus implied that we are to live by "every word that proceedeth out of the mouth of God" (Matt. 4:4). Paul was careful to preach "all the counsel of God" (Acts 20:27). "All Scripture is given by inspiration of God and is profitable" (2 Tim. 3:16).

If you ignore or neglect any part of the Bible, you invite trouble. You must read and study the whole book, and be able to rightly divide it (see 2 Tim. 2:15); that is, you must handle it accurately (see NASB). You should discern in the Bible what God says to different people at different times; there are passages that apply specifically to the Jews, or to the Gentiles, or to the church (1 Cor. 10:32). You must be careful to distinguish between them. Though all of the Bible was written for you, not all of it was written to you. False teachers, however, pick (out of context) only what they want, and often apply to believers today passages that were given only for ancient Israel.

John's second epistle gives further warning about false teachers (2 John 7–11). A Christian who meddles with these deceivers is in danger of losing his full reward (v. 8). You should not even say good-bye (which literally means "God be with you"). You are not to be rude or unkind, because that would not be Christian, but you are not to let them into your home to explain their views. Why? Because if you let them in, two consequences may follow: First, they will plant the seeds of false teaching in your mind, and Satan can water and nourish these seeds to produce bitter fruit. But even if this does not happen, by entertaining false teachers in your home you are giving them entrance into other homes! The deceiver will say to your neighbor down the street, "Mr. and Mrs. Smith let me into their home, and you know what good Christians they are!"

John has now concluded his message on fellowship and is about to begin his message on sonship. He has pointed out the contrasts between light and darkness (1 John 1:1—2:6), love and hatred (2:7–17), and truth and error (vv. 18–27). He has explained that a real Christian lives a life of obedience (walking in light, not darkness), love, and truth. It is impossible to live in fellowship with God if you are disobedient or hateful or untruthful. Any of these sins will lead you out of reality and into pretense. You will have an "artificial" life instead of an "authentic" life.

First John 2:28 and 29 are a bridge from the fellowship section into the sonship section ("born of God"); in these verses John used three words that ought to encourage us to live in fellowship with the Father, the Son, and the Spirit.

• **Abide.** This is a word we have met twice before. You must recognize the importance of abiding in Christ. In fact, this has been the theme of the first two chapters of this epistle. You abide in Christ by believing the truth, obeying the truth, and loving other Christians—"the brethren." Obedience—love—truth. If you are a believer and find yourself out of fellowship with God, it is because you have disobeyed His Word, lacked love for a brother, or believed a lie. The solution is to confess your sin instantly and to claim God's forgiveness (1 John 1:9).

• **Appear.** This is the first mention in this epistle of the promised return of Christ. The book of Revelation deals in detail with future events. The epistle (1 John 2:28–3:3; 4:17) merely mentions the return of Christ and a coming day of judgment.

Not all Bible students are agreed as to the details of future events, but evangelical Christians agree that Christ is returning for His church (1 Thess. 4:13–18). Though Christians will not then be judged for their sins, they will be judged on the basis of their faithfulness in serving Christ (1 Cor. 3:10–15). Those who have been faithful will receive rewards (4:5), and those who have not been faithful will lose rewards. This event is called "the judgment seat of Christ" (Rom. 14:10; 2 Cor. 5:10); do not confuse it with the "great white throne judgment" of unsaved people at the end of time (Rev. 20:11–15).

The fact that Jesus Christ may return at any moment ought to be an incentive for us to live in fellowship with Him and be obedient to His Word. For this reason, John used a third word:

• **Ashamed.** Some Christians will be "ashamed before him at his coming" (1 John 2:28). All believers are "accepted," but there is a difference between being "accepted" and being "acceptable." A disobedient child who goes out and gets dirty will be accepted when he comes home, but he will not be treated as though he were acceptable. "Therefore also we have as our ambition … to be pleasing to Him" (2 Cor. 5:9 NASB). A Christian who has not walked in fellowship with Christ in obedience, love, and truth will lose his rewards; and this will make him ashamed.

No matter in which direction a Christian looks, he finds reason to obey God. If he looks back, he sees Calvary, where Christ died for him. If he looks within, he sees the Holy Spirit, who lives within and teaches him the truth. If he looks around, he sees his Christian brethren, whom he loves; he also sees a world lost in sin, desperately needing his godly witness. And if he looks ahead, he sees the return of Christ! "And every man that hath this hope in him purifieth himself, even as he is pure" (1 John 3:3). The return of Christ is a great inspiration for godly living.

John has written about light and darkness, love and hatred, and truth and error, and in 1 John 2:29 he summed up the whole matter of Christian living in one phrase—"doing righteousness."

The life that is real is a life of doing, not simply talking ("If we say," 1 John 1:8—2:9) or giving mental assent that a doctrine is correct. "Not every one that saith unto me, 'Lord, Lord,' shall enter into the kingdom of heaven, but he that doeth the will of my Father which is in heaven" (Matt. 7:21). Christians do not simply believe the truth; they do it (1 John 1:6).

A person who professes to be a Christian, but who does not live in obedience, love, and truth, is either deceived or a deceiver. A child bears the nature of his father, and a person who has been "born of God" will reveal the characteristics of the heavenly Father. "Therefore be imitators of God, as beloved children" (Eph. 5:1 NASB). "As obedient children, not fashioning yourselves according to the former lusts in your ignorance: but as he which hath called you is holy, so be ye holy" (1 Peter 1:14–15).

A Sunday school class seemed to be having constant problems. The pastor and the superintendent met with the teacher and officers, but made no apparent progress. Then, one Sunday morning, the teacher of the class came down the aisle during the closing hymn of the service. "I suppose she wants to dedicate her life to the Lord," the pastor thought.

"Pastor," she said, "I want to confess Christ as my Savior. All these years I thought I was saved, but I wasn't. There was always something lacking in my life. The class problems were my problems, but now they've been solved. Now I know I'm saved."

"Test yourselves to see if you are in the faith; examine yourselves!" (2 Cor. 13:5 NASB). Does your life bear the marks of obedience, love, and truth? Is your Christian life something real—genuine—authentic? Or is it counterfeit?

It is a question of truth—or consequences!

And if you do not face the truth, you must pay the consequences!

# QUESTIONS FOR PERSONAL REFLECTION
# OR GROUP DISCUSSION

1. "It is not enough for a believer to walk in the light and to walk in love; he must also walk in truth." What does that mean to you?

2. Why is it so important for Christians to know what they believe and why?

3. Wiersbe lists three outstanding characteristics of the false teacher who is controlled by the "spirit of antichrist." Do you find this list helpful? Explain.

4. How is a desire to be with the people of God an evidence of a true Christian life?

5. What beliefs do all true Christians have in common?

6. What is essential about each part of this great assertion of faith: "Jesus Christ is God come in the flesh"?

7. Are you aware of the Holy Spirit guiding you? Explain.

8. "Though all of the Bible was written for you, not all of it was written to you." Do you agree? Explain.

9. Do you agree that Christians should not let false teachers into their homes? Why or why not?

10. What are a Christian's main protections against false teaching?

# Chapter Six

# THE PRETENDERS
## (1 John 3:1–10)

The United States Treasury Department has a special group of men whose job it is to track down counterfeiters. Naturally, these men need to know a counterfeit bill when they see it.

How do they learn to identify fake bills?

Oddly enough, they are not trained by spending hours examining counterfeit money. Rather, they study the real thing. They become so familiar with authentic bills that they can spot a counterfeit by looking at it or, often, simply by feeling it.

This is the approach in 1 John 3, which warns us that in today's world there are counterfeit Christians—"children of the devil" (1 John 3:10). But instead of listing the evil characteristics of Satan's children, the Scripture gives us a clear description of God's children. The contrast between the two is obvious.

The key verse of this chapter is 1 John 3:10: A true child of God practices righteousness and loves other Christians despite differences. First John 3:1–10 deals with the first topic, and 1 John 3:11–24 takes up the second.

Practicing righteousness and loving the brethren, of course, are not new themes. These two important subjects are treated in the first two chapters of this epistle, but in 1 John 3 the approach is different. In the first two chapters the emphasis was on fellowship: A Christian who is in fellowship with God will practice righteousness and will love the brethren. But in 1 John 3—5, the emphasis is on sonship: Because a Christian is "born of God," he will practice righteousness and will love the brethren.

"Born of God" is the idea that is basic to these chapters (see 1 John 2:29; 3:9; 4:7; 5:1, 4, 18).

When you read 1 John 3:1–10 in the Authorized Version, you may be startled by 1 John 3:6 and 9, which seem to contradict 1 John 1:8–9. The Authorized translation of the verbs here is not accurate. What the Greek text really says is "No one who abides in Him practices sin; no one who practices sin has seen Him or knows Him" (1 John 3:6). "No one who is born of God practices sin … he cannot practice sin because he is born of God" (v. 9). To "practice" sin is to sin consistently and as a way of life. It does not refer to committing an occasional sin. It is clear that no Christian is sinless (1 John 1:8–10), but God expects a true believer to sin less, not to sin habitually.

Every great personality mentioned in the Bible sinned at one time or another. Abraham lied about his wife (Gen. 12:10–20). Moses lost his temper and disobeyed God (Num. 20:7–13). Peter denied the Lord three times (Matt. 26:69–75). But sin was not the settled practice of these men. It was an incident in their lives, totally contrary to their normal habits. And when they sinned, they confessed it and asked God to forgive them.

An unsaved person (even if he professes to be a Christian but is a counterfeit) lives a life of habitual sin. Sin—especially the sin of unbelief— is the normal thing in his life (Eph. 2:1–3). He has no divine resources to draw on. His profession of faith, if any, is not real. This is the distinction in view in 1 John 3:1–10—a true believer does not live in habitual sin. He may commit sin—an occasional wrong act—but he will not practice sin—make a settled habit of it.

The difference is that a true Christian knows God. A counterfeit

Christian may talk about God and get involved in "religious activities," but he does not really know God. The person who has been "born of God" through faith in Christ knows God the Father, God the Son, and God the Holy Spirit. And because he knows them, he lives a life of obedience: He does not practice sin.

John gave us three reasons for a holy life.

## 1. GOD THE FATHER LOVES US (3:1–3)

God's love for us is unique. First John 3:1 may be translated, "Behold, what peculiar, out-of-this-world kind of love the Father has bestowed on us." While we were His enemies, God loved us and sent His Son to die for us!

The whole wonderful plan of salvation begins with the love of God.

Many translators add a phrase to 1 John 3:1: "That we should be called the sons of God, and we are." "Sons of God" is not simply a high-sounding name that we bear; it is a reality! We are God's children! We do not expect the world to understand this thrilling relationship, because it does not even understand God. Only a person who knows God through Christ can fully appreciate what it means to be called a child of God.

First John 3:1 tells us what we are, and 1 John 3:2 tells us what we shall be. The reference here, of course, is to the time of Christ's coming for His church. This was mentioned in 1 John 2:28 as an incentive for holy living, and now it is repeated.

God's love for us does not stop with the new birth. It continues throughout our lives and takes us right up to the return of Jesus Christ! When our Lord appears, all true believers will see Him and will become like Him (Phil. 3:20–21). This means, of course, that they will have new, glorified bodies, suited to heaven.

But the apostle did not stop here! He has told us what we are and what we shall be. Now, in 1 John 3:3, he told us what we should be. In view of the return of Jesus Christ, we should keep our lives clean.

All this is to remind us of the Father's love. Because the Father loved us and sent His Son to die for us, we are children of God. Because God loves us, He wants us to live with Him one day. Salvation, from start to finish, is an expression of the love of God. We are saved by the grace of God (Eph. 2:8–9; Titus 2:11–15), but the provision for our salvation was originated in the love of God. And since we have experienced the love of the Father, we have no desire to live in sin.

An unbeliever who sins is a creature sinning against his Creator. A Christian who sins is a child sinning against his Father. The unbeliever sins against law; the believer sins against love.

This reminds us of the meaning of the phrase so often repeated in the Bible: "the fear of the Lord." This phrase does not suggest that God's children live in an atmosphere of terror, "for God hath not given us the spirit of fear" (2 Tim. 1:7). Rather, it indicates that God's children hold their Father in reverence and will not deliberately disobey Him or try His patience.

A group of teenagers were enjoying a party, and someone suggested that they go to a certain restaurant for a good time.

"I'd rather you took me home," Jan said to her date. "My parents don't approve of that place."

"Afraid your father will hurt you?" one of the girls asked sarcastically.

"No," Jan replied, "I'm not afraid my father will hurt me, but I am afraid I might hurt him."

She understood the principle that a true child of God, who has experienced the love of God, has no desire to sin against that love.

## 2. GOD THE SON DIED FOR US (3:4–8)

John turned here from the future appearing of Jesus (1 John 3:2) to His past appearing (v. 5, where the word *manifest* means "appear"). John gave two reasons why Jesus came and died: (1) to take away our sins (vv. 4–6), and (2) to destroy the works of the Devil (vv. 7–8). For a child of God to sin indicates that he does not understand or appreciate what Jesus did for him on the cross.

**(1) Christ appeared to take away our sins (vv. 4–6).** There are several definitions of sin in the Bible: "Whatsoever is not of faith is sin" (Rom. 14:23). "The thought of foolishness is sin" (Prov. 24:9). "Therefore to him that knoweth to do good, and doeth it not, to him it is sin" (James 4:17). "All unrighteousness is sin" (1 John 5:17). But John's epistle defines sin as lawlessness (3:4 NASB). It views sin as defilement (1:9—2:2), but here it views it as defiance.

The emphasis here is not on sins (plural), but on sin (singular): "Whosoever practices sin." Sins are the fruit, but sin is the root.

That God is love does not mean He has no rules and regulations for His family. "And hereby we do know that we know him, if we keep his commandments" (1 John 2:3). "And whatsoever we ask, we receive of him, because we keep his commandments, and do those things that are pleasing in his sight" (3:22). "By this we know that we love the children of God, when we love God and keep his commandments" (5:2).

God's children are not in bondage to the Old Testament law, for Christ has set us free and has given us liberty (Gal. 5:1–6). But God's children are not to be lawless, either! They are "not without law to God, but under the law to Christ" (1 Cor. 9:21).

Sin is basically a matter of the will. For us to assert our will against God's will is rebellion, and rebellion is the root of sin. It is not simply that sin reveals itself in lawless behavior, but that the very essence of sin is lawlessness. No matter what his outward action may be, a sinner's inward attitude is one of rebellion.

Little Judy was riding in the car with her father. She decided to stand up in the front seat. Her father commanded her to sit down and put on the seat belt, but she declined. He told her a second time, and again she refused.

"If you don't sit down immediately, I'll pull over to the side of the road and spank you!" Dad finally said, and at this the little girl obeyed. But in a few minutes she said quietly, "Daddy, I'm still standing up inside."

Lawlessness! Rebellion! Even though there was constraint from the outside, there was still rebellion on the inside, and this attitude is the essence of sin.

But after a person has become a child of God, born again by faith in Jesus Christ, he cannot practice lawlessness! For one thing, Jesus Christ was without sin, and to abide in Him means to be identified with the One who is sinless. And even more than that, Jesus Christ died to take away our sins! If we know the Person of Christ, and if we have shared in the blessing of His death, we cannot deliberately disobey God. The whole work of the cross is denied when a professed Christian practices deliberate sin. This is one reason why Paul called such people "enemies of the cross of Christ" (Phil. 3:18–19).

"Whosoever abideth in him" does not practice sin (1 John 3:6). "Abide" was one of John's favorite words. To abide in Christ means to be in fellowship with Him, to allow nothing to come between ourselves and Christ. Sonship (being born of God) brings about our union with Christ, but fellowship makes possible our communion with Christ. It is this communion (abiding) with Christ that keeps us from deliberately disobeying His Word.

A person who deliberately and habitually sins is proving that he does not know Christ and therefore cannot be abiding in Him.

There is more in the death of Christ on the cross than simply our salvation from judgment, as wonderful as that is. Through His death, Christ broke the power of the sin principle in our lives. The theme of Romans 6—8 is this identification with Christ in His death and resurrection. Christ not only died for me, but I died with Christ! Now I can yield myself to Him and sin will not have dominion over me.

**(2) Christ appeared to destroy the works of the Devil (vv. 7–8).** The logic here is clear: If a man knows God, he will obey God; if he belongs to the Devil, he will obey the Devil. John accepted the reality of a personal Devil.

This enemy has many different names in Scripture: Satan (adversary, enemy), the Devil (accuser), Abaddon or Apollyon (destroyer), the Prince of this World, the Dragon, and so forth. Whatever name you call him, keep in mind that his chief activity is to oppose Christ and God's people.

The contrast here is between Christ (who has no sin, 1 John 3:5) and the Devil (who can do nothing but sin).

The origin of Satan is a mystery. Many scholars believe he was once one of the highest angels, placed by God over the earth and over the other angels, and that he sinned against God and was cast down (Isa. 14:9–17; Ezek. 28:12–14).

Satan is not eternal, as is God, for he is a created being. He was not created sinful. His present nature is a result of his past rebellion. Satan is not like God: He is not all-powerful, all-knowing, or everywhere present. However, he is assisted by an army of spirit creatures known as demons, who make it possible for him to work in many places at one time (Eph. 6:10–12).

Satan is a rebel, but Christ is the obedient Son of God. Christ was "obedient unto death, even the death of the cross" (Phil. 2:8). Christ is God but was willing to become a servant. Satan was a servant and wanted to become God. From the beginning of his career, Satan has been a sinner, and Christ came to destroy the works of the Devil.

"Destroy" (1 John 3:8) does not mean "annihilate." Satan is certainly still at work today! "Destroy," here, means "to render inoperative, to rob of power." Satan has not been annihilated, but his power has been reduced and his weapons have been impaired. He is still a mighty foe, but he is no match for the power of God.

Jesus compared this world to a palace that contains many valuable goods. A strong man is guarding this palace (Luke 11:14–23). Satan is the strong man, and his "goods" are lost men and women. The only way to release the "goods" is to bind the strong man, and that is just what Jesus did on the cross. Jesus, in coming to earth, invaded Satan's "palace." When He died, He broke Satan's power and captured his goods! Each time a lost sinner is won to Christ, more of Satan's "spoils" are taken from him.

For many months after the close of World War II, Japanese troops were discovered hidden in the caves and jungles of the Pacific islands. Some of these stragglers were living like frightened savages; they didn't know the war was over. Once they understood that it was no longer necessary for them to fight, they surrendered.

Christians may rest in the truth that Satan is a defeated enemy. He may still win a few battles here and there, but he has already lost the war! Sentence has been pronounced on him, but it will be awhile before the punishment is meted out. A person who knows Christ, and who has been delivered from the bondage of sin through Christ's death on the cross, has no desire to obey Satan and live like a rebel.

"Little children, let no man deceive you!" Counterfeit Christians were trying to convince true believers that a person could be "saved" and still practice sin. John did not deny that Christians sin, but he did deny that Christians can live in sin. A person who can enjoy deliberate sin and who does not feel convicted or experience God's chastening had better examine himself to see whether or not he is really born of God.

## 3. God the Holy Spirit Lives in Us (3:9–10)

"Whosoever is born of God does not practice sin!"

Why? Because he has a new nature within him, and that new nature cannot sin. John called this new nature God's "seed."

When a person receives Christ as his Savior, tremendous spiritual changes take place in him. He is given a new standing before God, being accepted as righteous in God's sight. This new standing is called "justification." It never changes and is never lost.

The new Christian is also given a new position: He is set apart for God's own purposes to live for His glory. This new position is called "sanctification," and it has a way of changing from day to day. On some days we are much closer to Christ and obey Him much more readily.

But perhaps the most dramatic change in a new believer is what we call "regeneration." He is "born again" into the family of God. (*Re-* means "again," and *generation* means "birth.")

Justification means a new standing before God, sanctification means being set apart to God, and regeneration means a new nature—God's nature (see 2 Peter 1:4).

The only way to enter God's family is by trusting Christ and experiencing this new birth. "Whosoever believeth that Jesus is the Christ is born of God" (1 John 5:1).

Physical life produces only physical life; spiritual life produces spiritual life. "That which is born of the flesh is flesh; and that which is born of the Spirit is spirit" (John 3:6). Christians have been born again, "not of corruptible seed, but of incorruptible, by the word of God, which liveth and abideth forever" (1 Peter 1:23). A Christian's "spiritual parents," so to speak, are the Word of God and the Spirit of God. The Spirit of God uses the Word of God to convict of sin and to reveal the Savior.

We are saved by faith (Eph. 2:8–9), and "faith cometh by hearing, and hearing by the word of God" (Rom. 10:17). In the miracle of the new birth, the Holy Spirit imparts new life—God's life—to a believing sinner, and as a result the individual is born into the family of God.

Just as physical children bear the nature of their parents, so God's spiritual children bear His nature. The divine "seed" is in them. A Christian has an old nature from his physical birth and a new nature from his spiritual birth. The New Testament contrasts these two natures and gives them various names:

| Old Nature | New Nature |
|---|---|
| "our old man" (Rom. 6:6) | "the new man" (Col. 3:10) |
| "the flesh" (Gal. 5:24) | "the Spirit" (Gal. 5:17) |
| "corruptible seed" (1 Peter 1:23) | "God's seed" (1 John 3:9) |

The old nature produces sin, but the new nature leads one into a holy life. A Christian's responsibility is to live according to his new nature, not the old nature.

One way to illustrate this is by contrasting the "outer man" with the "inner man" (2 Cor. 4:16 NASB). The physical man needs food, and so does the inner, or spiritual man. "Man shall not live by bread alone, but by every word that proceedeth out of the mouth of God" (Matt. 4:4). Unless a Christian spends time daily in meditating on the Word of God, his inner man will lack power.

A converted Native American explained, "I have two dogs living in me—a mean dog and a good dog. They are always fighting. The mean dog wants me to do bad things, and the good dog wants me to do good things. Do you want to know which dog wins? The one I feed the most!"

A Christian who feeds the new nature from the Word of God will have power to live a godly life. We are to "make not provision for the flesh, to fulfill the lusts thereof" (Rom. 13:14).

The physical man needs cleansing, and so does the inner man. We wash our hands and face frequently. A believer should look into the mirror of God's Word daily (James 1:22–25) and examine himself. He must confess his sins and claim God's forgiveness (1 John 1:9). Otherwise the inner man will become unclean, and this uncleanness will breed infection and "spiritual sickness."

Unconfessed sin is the first step in what the Bible calls "backsliding"—gradually moving away from a close walk with Christ into a life filled with the alien world in which we live.

God's promise "I will heal your backslidings" (Jer. 3:22) implies that backsliding resembles physical sickness. First is the secret invasion of the body by a disease germ. Then infection follows and there is a gradual decline: no pep, no appetite, no interest in normal activities. Then comes the collapse!

Spiritual decline works in a similar way. First sin invades us. Instead of fighting it, we yield to it (see James 1:14) and infection sets in. A gradual decline follows. We lose our appetite for spiritual things, we become listless and even irritable, and finally we collapse.

The only remedy is to confess and forsake our sin and turn to Christ for cleansing and healing.

The inner man not only needs food and cleansing, but he also needs exercise. "Exercise thyself … unto godliness" (1 Tim. 4:7). A person who eats but does not exercise will become overweight; a person who exercises without eating will kill himself. There must be proper balance.

"Spiritual exercise" for a believer includes sharing Christ with others, doing good works in Christ's name, and helping to build up other believers. Each Christian has at least one spiritual gift, which he is to use for the good of the church (1 Cor. 12:1–11). "As each one has received a special gift, employ it in serving one another, as good stewards of the manifold grace of God" (1 Peter 4:10 NASB).

Here is a vivid commentary on this whole process of temptation and sin:

> Let no one say when he is tempted, "I am being tempted by God"; for God cannot be tempted by evil, and He Himself does not tempt anyone. But each one is tempted when he is carried away and enticed by his own lust. Then when lust has conceived, it gives birth to sin; and when sin is accomplished, it brings forth death. (James 1:13–15 NASB)

Temptation appeals to our basic natural desires. There is nothing sinful about our desires, but temptation gives us an opportunity to satisfy these desires in an evil way. It is not a sin to be hungry, but it is a sin to satisfy hunger out of the will of God. This was the first temptation Satan hurled at Jesus (Matt. 4:1–4).

The two terms, "carried away" and "enticed" (James 1:14 NASB), both relate to hunting or fishing: the putting of bait in a trap or on a hook. The animal (or fish) comes along, and his natural desires attract him to the bait. But in taking the bait, he gets caught in the trap, or hooked. And the end is death.

Satan baits his traps with pleasures that appeal to the old nature, the flesh. But none of his bait appeals to the new divine nature within a Christian. If a believer yields to his old nature, he will hanker for the bait, take it, and sin. But if he follows the leanings of his new nature, he will refuse the bait and obey God. "This I say then, walk in the Spirit, and ye shall not fulfill the lust of the flesh" (Gal. 5:16).

Yielding to sin is the distinguishing mark of "the children of the devil" (1 John 3:10). They profess, or claim, one thing, but they practice another. Satan is a liar and the father of lies (John 8:44), and his children are like their father. "He that saith, 'I know [God],' and keepeth not his commandments, is a liar, and the truth is not in him" (1 John 2:4). The children of the Devil try to deceive God's children into thinking that a person can be a Christian and still practice sin. "Little children, let no man deceive you; he that doeth righteousness is righteous, even as he [God] is righteous" (3:7).

False teachers in John's day taught that a Christian did not have to worry about sin, because only the body sinned and what the body did in no way affected the spirit. Some of them went so far as to teach that sin is natural to the body, because the body is sinful.

The New Testament exposes the foolishness of such excuses for sin.

To begin with, "the old nature" is not the body. The body itself is neutral: It can be used either by the old sinful nature or by the new divine nature. "Therefore do not let sin reign in your mortal body so that you obey its lusts, and do not go on presenting the members of your body to sin as instruments of unrighteousness; but present yourselves to God as those [who are] alive from the dead, and your members as instruments of righteousness to God" (Rom. 6:12–13 NASB).

How does a child of God go about overcoming the desires of the old nature? He must begin each day by yielding his body to God as a living sacrifice (Rom. 12:1). He must spend time reading and studying the Word of God, "feeding" his new nature. He must take time to pray, asking God to fill him with the Holy Spirit and give him power to serve Christ and glorify Him.

As he goes through the day, a believer must depend on the power of the Spirit in the inner man. When temptations come, he must immediately turn to Christ for victory.

The Word of God in his heart will help to keep him from sin if only he will turn to Christ. "Thy word have I hid in mine heart, that I might not sin against thee" (Ps. 119:11). If he does sin, he must instantly confess to God and claim forgiveness. But it is not necessary for him to sin. By yielding his body to the Holy Spirit within him, he will receive the power he needs to overcome the tempter.

A good practice is to claim God's promise: "No temptation has overtaken you but such as is common to man; and God is faithful, who will not allow you to be tempted beyond what you are able, but with the temptation will provide the way of escape also, so that you will be able to endure it" (1 Cor. 10:13 NASB).

A Sunday school teacher was explaining the Christian's two natures—the old and the new—to a class of teenagers.

"Our old nature came from Adam," he explained, "and our new nature comes from Christ, who is called 'the Last Adam.'" He had the class read 1 Corinthians 15:45: "So also it is written, 'The first man, Adam, became a living soul.' The Last Adam became a life-giving spirit" (NASB).

"This means there are two 'Adams' living in me," said one of the teenagers.

"That's right," the teacher replied. "And what is the practical value of this truth?"

The class was silent for a moment, and then a student spoke up.

"This idea of the 'two Adams' really helps me in fighting temptation," he said. "When temptation comes knocking at my door, if I send the first Adam to answer, I'll sin. But if I send the Last Adam, I'll get victory."

A true believer does not practice sin; a counterfeit believer cannot help but practice sin because he does not have God's new nature within him. The true believer also loves other Christians, which is discussed in detail in 1 John 3:11–24.

But these words were not written so that you and I might check on other people. They were inspired so that we may examine ourselves. Each of us must answer honestly before God:

1. Do I have the divine nature within me, or am I merely pretending to be a Christian?

2. Do I cultivate this divine nature by daily Bible reading and prayer?

3. Has any unconfessed sin defiled my inner man? Am I willing to confess and forsake it?

4. Do I allow my old nature to control my thoughts and desires, or does the divine nature rule me?

5. When temptation comes, do I "play with it," or do I flee from it? Do I immediately yield to the divine nature within me?

The life that is real is honest with God about these vital issues.

# QUESTIONS FOR PERSONAL REFLECTION
# OR GROUP DISCUSSION

1. "It is clear that no Christian is sinless, but God expects a true believer to sin less." What does that mean?

2. How does knowing that God deeply loves us motivate us to live a holy life?

3. "Christ not only died for me, but I died with Christ!" What does that mean?

4. What is justification? What is sanctification? How is each of these at work in your life?

5. What is regeneration?

6. What does it mean to say that "Whosoever is born of God does not practice sin"?

7. Why does unconfessed sin lead to "backsliding"?

8. How does memorizing Scripture help keep a Christian from sinning?

9. What healthy habits (such as meditating on God's Word, praying, or serving other people) do you particularly need to focus on increasing in your life in order to uproot habits of sin?

# Chapter Seven

# LOVE OR DEATH

## (1 John 3:11–24)

John's letter has been compared to a spiral staircase because he kept returning to the same three topics: love, obedience, and truth. Though these themes recur, it is not true that they are merely repetitious. Each time we return to a topic, we look at it from a different point of view and are taken more deeply into it.

We have already learned about our love for other believers—"the brethren" (1 John 2:7–11)—but the emphasis in 1 John 2 is on fellowship. A believer who is "walking in the light" will evidence that fact by loving the brethren. In our present section, the emphasis is on his relationship with other believers.

Christians love one another because they have all been born of God, which makes them all brothers and sisters in Christ.

Obedience and love are both evidences of sonship and brotherhood. We have been reminded that a true child of God practices righteousness (1 John 3:1–10), and now we shall look into the matter of love for the brethren (vv. 11–24). This truth is first stated in the negative: "Whosoever doeth not righteousness is not of God, neither he that loveth not his brother" (v. 10).

A striking difference should be noted between the earlier and the present treatment of love for the brethren. In the section on fellowship (1 John 2:7–11), we are told that loving the brethren is a matter of light and darkness. If we do not love one another, we cannot walk in the light, no matter how loud our profession. But in this section on brotherhood (3:11–24), the epistle probes much deeper. We are told that loving the brethren is a matter of life and death. "He that loveth not his brother abideth in death" (v. 14).

When it comes to this matter of love, there are four possible "levels of relationship," so to speak, on which a person may live: murder (1 John 3:11–12), hatred (vv. 13–15), indifference (vv. 16–17), and Christian compassion (vv. 18–24).

The first two are not Christian at all, the third is less than Christian, and only the last is compatible with true Christian love.

## 1. Murder (3:11–12)

Murder, of course, is the lowest level on which one may live in relationship to someone else. It is the level on which Satan himself exists. The Devil was a murderer from the beginning of his fallen career (John 8:44), but Christians have heard, from the beginning of their experience, that they are to "love one another." John emphasized origins: "Go back to the beginning." If our spiritual experience originates with the Father, we must love one another. But if it originates with Satan, we will hate one another. "Let that therefore abide in you which ye have heard from the beginning" (1 John 2:24).

Cain is an example of a life of hatred; we find the record in Genesis 4:1–16. It is important to note that Cain and Abel, being brothers, had the same parents, and they both brought sacrifices to God. Cain is not presented as an atheist; he is presented as a worshipper. And this is the point: Children of the Devil masquerade as true believers. They attend religious gatherings, as Cain did. They may even bring offerings. But these actions in themselves are not valid proof that a man is born of God. The real test is his love for the brethren—and here Cain failed.

Every man has a "spiritual lineage" as well as a physical, and Cain's "spiritual father" was the Devil. This does not mean, of course, that Satan literally fathered Cain. It means, rather, that Cain's attitudes and actions originated with Satan. Cain was a murderer and a liar like Satan (John 8:44). He murdered his brother, and then he lied about it. "And the LORD said unto Cain, Where is Abel thy brother? And he said, I know not" (Gen. 4:9).

In contrast to this, God is love (1 John 4:8) and truth (John 14:6; 1 John 5:6); therefore, those who belong to God's family practice love and truth.

The difference between Cain's offering and Abel's offering was faith (Heb. 11:4), and faith is always based on the revelation God has given (Rom. 10:17). It seems clear that God must have given definite instructions concerning how He was to be worshipped. Cain rejected God's Word and decided to worship in his own way. This shows his relationship to Satan, for Satan is always interested in turning people away from the revealed will of God. The Devil's "Yea, hath God said?" (Gen. 3:1) was the beginning of trouble for Cain's parents and for all mankind since.

We are not told by what outward sign the Lord accepted Abel's sacrifice and rejected Cain's. It may be that He sent fire from heaven to consume Abel's sacrifice of an animal and its blood. But we are told the results: Abel went away from the altar with God's witness of acceptance in his heart, but Cain went away angry and disappointed (Gen. 4:4–6). God warned Cain that sin was crouching at the door like a dangerous beast (v. 7) but promised that if Cain would obey God, he, like Abel, would enjoy peace.

Instead of heeding God's warning, Cain listened to Satan's voice and plotted to kill his brother. His envy had turned to anger and hatred. He knew that he was evil and that his brother was righteous. Rather than repent, as God commanded him to do, he decided to destroy his brother.

Centuries later, the Pharisees did the same thing to Jesus (Mark 15:9–10), and Jesus called them, too, children of the Devil (John 8:44).

Cain's attitude represents the attitude of the present world system (1 John 3:13). The world hates Christ (John 15:18–25) for the same reason Cain hated Abel: Christ shows up the world's sin and reveals its true nature. When the world, like Cain, comes face-to-face with reality and truth, it can make only one of two decisions: Repent and change, or destroy the one who is exposing it.

Satan is the "prince of this world" (John 14:30), and he controls it through murder and lies. How horrible to live on the same level as Satan!

A hunter took refuge in a cave during a rainstorm. After he had dried out a bit, he decided to investigate his temporary home and turned on his flashlight. Imagine his surprise when he discovered he was sharing the cave with an assortment of spiders, lizards, and snakes! His exit was a fast one.

If the unsaved world could only see, it would realize that it is living on the low level of murder and lies, surrounded by that old serpent Satan and all his demonic armies. Like Cain, the people of the world try to cover up their true nature with religious rites, but they lack faith in God's Word. People who continue to live on this level will eventually be cast into outer darkness with Satan to suffer apart from God forever.

## 2. HATRED (3:13–15)

At this point, you are probably thinking, "But I have never murdered anyone!" And to this statement, God replies, "Yes, but remember that to a Christian hatred is the same as murder" (1 John 3:15; cf. Matt. 5:22). The only difference between Level 1 and Level 2 is the outward act of taking life. The inward intent is the same.

A visitor at the zoo was chatting with the keeper of the lion house.

"I have a cat at home," said the visitor, "and your lions act just like my cat. Look at them sleeping so peacefully! It seems a shame that you have to put those beautiful creatures behind bars."

"My friend," the keeper laughed, "these may look like your cat, but their disposition is radically different. There's murder in their hearts. You'd better be glad the bars are there."

The only reason some people have never actually murdered anyone is because of the "bars" that have been put up: the fear of arrest and shame, the penalties of the law, and the possibility of death. But we are going to be judged by "the law of liberty" (James 2:12). The question is not so much "What did you do?" but "What did you want to do? What would you have done if you had been at liberty to do as you pleased?" This is why Jesus equated hatred with murder (Matt. 5:21–26) and lust with adultery (vv. 27–30).

This does not mean, of course, that hatred in the heart does the same amount of damage, or involves the same degree of guilt, as actual murder. Your neighbor would rather you hate him than kill him! But in God's sight, hatred is the moral equivalent of murder, and if left unbridled it leads to murder. A Christian has passed from death to life (John 5:24), and the proof of this is that he loves the brethren. When he belonged to the world system, he hated God's people, but now that he belongs to God, he loves them.

These verses (1 John 3:14–15), like those that deal with habitual sin in a believer (1:5—2:6), concern a settled habit of life: A believer is in the practice of loving the brethren, even though on occasion he may be angry with a brother (Matt. 5:22–24). Occasional incidents of anger do not nullify the principle. If anything, they prove it true because a believer out of fellowship with his fellow Christians is a miserable person! His feelings make clear to him that something is wrong.

Notice another fact: We are not told that murderers cannot be saved. The apostle Paul himself took a hand in the stoning of Stephen (Acts 7:57–60) and admitted that his vote helped to put innocent people to death (26:9–11; 1 Tim. 1:12–15). But in His grace God saved Paul.

The issue here is not whether a murderer can become a Christian, but whether a man can continue being a murderer and still be a Christian. The answer is no. "And ye know that no murderer hath eternal life abiding in him" (1 John 3:15). The murderer did not once have eternal life and then lose it; he never had eternal life at all.

The fact that you have never actually murdered anyone should not make you proud or complacent. Have you ever harbored hatred in your heart?

Hatred does the hater far more damage than it does anyone else (Matt. 5:21–26). Jesus said that anger put a man in danger of facing the local court. Calling a brother an "empty-headed fool" put him in danger of the Sanhedrin, the highest Jewish council. But calling him a "cursed fool" put him in danger of eternal judgment in hell. Hatred that is not confessed and forsaken actually puts a man into a spiritual and emotional prison (v. 25)!

The antidote for hatred is love. "Hateful and hating one another" is the normal experience of an unsaved person (Titus 3:3). But when a hateful heart opens to Jesus Christ, it becomes a loving heart. Then instead of wanting to "murder" others through hatred, one wants to love them and share with them the message of eternal life.

Evangelist John Wesley was stopped one night by a highwayman who robbed the Methodist leader of all his money. Wesley said to the man, "If the day should come that you desire to leave this evil way and live for God, remember that 'the blood of Jesus Christ cleanses from all sin.'"

Some years later, Wesley was stopped by a man after a church service. "Do you remember me?" the man asked. "I robbed you one night, and you told me that the blood of Jesus Christ cleanses from all sin. I have trusted Christ, and He has changed my life."

## 3. INDIFFERENCE (3:16–17)

But the test of Christian love is not simply failure to do evil to others. Love also involves doing them good. Christian love is both positive and negative. "Cease to do evil; learn to do well" (Isa. 1:16–17).

Cain is our example of false love; Christ is the example of true Christian love. Jesus gave His life for us that we may experience truth. Every Christian knows John 3:16, but how many of us pay much attention to 1 John 3:16? It is wonderful to experience the blessing of John 3:16, but it is even more wonderful to share that experience by obeying 1 John 3:16: Christ "laid down life for us: and we ought to lay down our lives for the brethren."

Christian love involves sacrifice and service. Christ did not simply talk about His love; He died to prove it (Rom. 5:6–10). Jesus was not killed as a martyr; He willingly laid down His life (John 10:11–18; 15:13). "Self-preservation" is the first law of physical life, but "self-sacrifice" is the first law of spiritual life.

But God does not ask us to lay down our lives. He simply asks us to help a brother in need. John wisely turned from "the brethren" in 1 John 3:16 to the singular, "his brother," in 1 John 3:17.

It is easy for us to talk about "loving the brethren" and to neglect to help a single other believer. Christian love is personal and active.

This is what Jesus had in mind in the parable of the good Samaritan (Luke 10:25–37). A lawyer wanted to talk about an abstract subject: "Who is my neighbor?" But Jesus focused attention on one man in need, and changed the question to "To whom can I be a neighbor?"

Two friends were attending a conference on evangelism. During one of the sessions, Larry missed Pete. At luncheon, when he saw Pete, he said, "I missed you at the ten o'clock session. It was really terrific! Where were you?"

"I was in the lobby talking to a bellhop about Christ. I led him to the Lord," said Pete.

There is nothing wrong with attending conferences, but it is easy to forget the individual and his needs while discussing generalities. The test of Christian love is not in loud professions about loving the whole church, but in quietly helping a brother who is in need. If we do not even help a brother, it is not likely we would "lay down our lives" for "the brethren."

A man does not have to murder in order to sin; hatred is murder in his heart. But a man need not even hate his brother to be guilty of sin. All he has to do is ignore him or be indifferent toward his needs. A believer who has material goods and can relieve his brother's needs ought to do it. To "close the door of his heart" on his brother is a kind of murder!

If I am going to help my brother, I must meet three conditions. First, I must have the means necessary to meet his need. Second, I must know that the need exists. Third, I must be loving enough to want to share.

A believer who is too poor to help or who is ignorant of his brother's need is not condemned. But a believer who hardens his heart against his needy brother is condemned. One reason Christians should work is so that they may be able "to give to him that needeth" (Eph. 4:28).

In these days of multiplied social agencies, it is easy for Christians to forget their obligations. "So then, while we have opportunity, let us do good to all people, and especially to those who are of the household of the faith" (Gal. 6:10 NASB).

This "doing good" need not be in terms of money or material supplies. It may include personal service and the giving of oneself to others. There are many individuals in our churches who lack love and would welcome friendship.

A young mother admitted in a testimony meeting that she never seemed to find time for her own personal devotions. She had several little children to care for, and the hours melted away.

Imagine her surprise when two of the women from the church appeared at her front door.

"We've come to take over," they explained. "You go into the bedroom and get started on your devotions." After several days of this kind of help, the young mother was able to develop her devotional life so that the daily demands on her time no longer upset her.

If we want to experience and enjoy the love of God in our own hearts, we must love others, even to the point of sacrifice. Being indifferent to a brother's needs means robbing ourselves of what we need even more: the love of God in our hearts. It is a matter of love or death!

## 4. CHRISTIAN LOVE (3:18–24)

True Christian love means loving in deed and in truth. The opposite of "in deed" is "in word," and the opposite of "in truth" is "in tongue." Here is an example of love "in word": "If a brother or sister is without clothing and in need of daily food, and one of you says to them, 'Go in peace, be warmed and be filled,' and yet you do not give them what is necessary for their body, what use is that?" (James 2:15–16 NASB).

To love "in word" means simply to talk about a need, but to love "in deed" means to do something about meeting it. You may think, because you have discussed a need, or even prayed about it, that you have done your duty, but love involves more than words—it calls for sacrificial deeds.

To love "in tongue" is the opposite of to love "in truth." It means to love insincerely. To love "in truth" means to love a person genuinely from the heart and not just from the tongue. People are attracted by genuine love, but repelled by the artificial variety. One reason why sinners were attracted to Jesus (Luke 15:1–2) was because they were sure He loved them sincerely.

"But does it not cost a great deal for the believer to exercise this kind of love?"

Yes, it does. It cost Jesus Christ His life. But the wonderful benefits that come to you as by-products of this love more than compensate for any sacrifice you make. To be sure, you do not love others because you want to get something in return, but the Bible principle "Give and it shall be given unto you" (Luke 6:38) applies to love as well as to money.

John named three wonderful blessings that will come to a believer who practices Christian love.

**(1) Assurance (vv. 19–20).** A believer's relationship with others affects his relationship with God. A man who is not right with his brother should go settle the matter before he offers his sacrifice on the altar (see Matt. 5:23–24). A Christian who practices love grows in his understanding of God's truth and enjoys a heart filled with confidence before God.

A "condemning heart" is one that robs a believer of peace. An "accusing conscience" is another way to describe it. Sometimes the heart accuses us wrongly because it "is deceitful above all things, and desperately wicked: who can know it?" (Jer. 17:9). The answer to that question is, "God knows the heart!" More than one Christian has accused himself falsely or been harder on himself than necessary, but God will never make such a mistake. A Christian who walks in love has a heart open to God ("God is love") and knows that God never judges wrongly.

John may have remembered two incidents from Jesus' life on earth that illustrate this important principle. When Jesus visited Bethany, He stayed at the home of Mary and Martha (Luke 10:38–42). Martha was busy preparing the meal, but Mary sat at His feet and listened to Him teach. Martha criticized both Mary and Jesus, but Jesus knew Mary's heart and defended her.

The apostle Peter wept bitterly after he had denied his Lord, and no doubt he was filled with remorse and repentance for his sin. But Jesus knew that Peter had repented, and after His resurrection the Lord sent a special message to Peter that must have assured the hot-headed fisherman that he was forgiven (Mark 16:7). Peter's heart may have condemned him, for he knew he had denied the Lord three times, but God was greater than his heart. Jesus, knowing all things, gave Peter just the assurance he needed.

Be careful lest the Devil accuse you and rob you of your confidence (Rev. 12:10). Once you confess your sin and it is forgiven, you need not allow it to accuse you anymore. Peter was able to face the Jews and say, "But ye denied the Holy One and the Just" (Acts 3:14) because his own sin of denying Christ had been taken care of and was forgiven and forgotten.

No Christian should treat sin lightly, but no Christian should be harder on himself than God is. There is a morbid kind of self-examination and self-condemnation that is not spiritual. If you are practicing genuine love for the brethren, your heart must be right before God, for the Holy

Spirit would not "shed abroad" His love in you if there were habitual sin in your heart. When you grieve the Spirit, you "turn off" the supply of God's love (Eph. 4:30—5:2).

**(2) Answered prayer (vv. 21–22).** Love for the brethren produces confidence toward God, and confidence toward God gives you boldness in asking for what you need. This does not mean that you earn answers to prayer by loving the brethren. Rather, it means that your love for the brethren proves that you are living in the will of God where God can answer your prayer. "And whatsoever we ask, we receive of him, because we keep his commandments" (1 John 3:22). Love is the fulfilling of God's law (Rom. 13:8–10); therefore, when you love the brethren, you are obeying His commandments and He is able to answer your requests.

A believer's relationship to the brethren cannot be divorced from his prayer life. If husbands and wives are not obeying God's Word, for example, their prayers will be hindered (1 Peter 3:7).

An evangelist had preached on the Christian home. After the meeting a father approached him.

"I've been praying for a wayward son for years," said the father, "and God has not answered my prayers."

The evangelist read Psalm 66:18—"If I regard iniquity in my heart, the Lord will not hear me."

"Be honest with yourself and the Lord," he said. "Is there anything between you and another Christian that needs to be settled?"

The father hesitated, then said, "Yes, I'm afraid there is. I've harbored resentment in my heart against another man in this church."

"Then go make it right," counseled the evangelist, and he prayed with the man. Before the campaign was over, the father saw his wayward son come back to the Lord.

These verses do not, of course, give us all the conditions for answered prayer, but they emphasize the importance of obedience. One great secret of answered prayer is obedience, and the secret of obedience is love. "If ye love me, keep my commandments" (John 14:15). "If ye abide in me, and my words abide in you, ye shall ask what ye will, and it shall be done unto you.… If ye keep my commandments, ye shall abide in my love" (15:7, 10).

It is possible, of course, to keep God's commandments in a spirit of fear or servitude rather than in a spirit of love. This was the sin of the elder brother in the parable of the prodigal son (Luke 15:24–32). A believer should keep His Father's commandments because this pleases Him. A Christian who lives to please God will discover that God finds ways to please His child. "Delight thyself also in the LORD, and he shall give thee the desires of thine heart" (Ps. 37:4). When our delight is in the love of God, our desires will be in the will of God.

**(3) Abiding (vv. 23–24).** When a scribe asked Jesus to name the greatest commandment, He replied, "Thou shalt love the Lord thy God." Then He added a second commandment: "Thou shalt love thy neighbor as thyself" (Matt. 22:34–40). But God also gives us one commandment that takes in both God and man: "Believe in the name of His Son Jesus Christ, and love one another" (1 John 3:23 NASB). Faith toward God and love toward man sum up a Christian's obligations. Christianity is "faith which worketh by love" (Gal. 5:6).

Faith toward God and love toward men are two sides of the same coin. It is easy to emphasize faith—correct doctrine—and to neglect love. On the other hand, some say doctrine is not important and that love is our main responsibility. Both doctrine and love are important. When a person is justified by faith, he should know that the love of God is being shed abroad in his heart (Rom. 5:1–5).

"Abiding in Christ" is a key experience for a believer who wants to have confidence toward God and enjoy answers to prayer. Jesus, in His message to the disciples in the upper room (John 15:1–14) illustrated "abiding." He compared His followers to the branches of a vine. So long as the branch draws its strength from the vine, it produces fruit. But if it separates itself from the vine, it withers and dies.

Jesus was not talking about salvation; He was talking about fruit-bearing. The instant a sinner trusts Christ, he enters into union with Christ, but maintaining communion is a moment-by-moment responsibility. Abiding depends on our obeying His Word and keeping clean (John 15:3, 10).

As we have seen, when a believer walks in love, he finds it easy to obey God, and therefore he maintains a close communion with God. "If a man love me, he will keep my words; and my Father will love him, and we will come unto him and make our abode with him" (John 14:23).

The Holy Spirit is mentioned by name in 1 John for the first time in 3:24. John introduced us to the Holy One (1 John 2:20) with emphasis on the Spirit's anointing and teaching ministry. (This parallels John 14:26 and 16:13–14.) But the Holy One is also the abiding Spirit (1 John 3:24; 4:13). When a believer obeys God and loves the brethren, the indwelling Holy Spirit gives him peace and confidence. The Holy Spirit abides with him forever (John 14:16), but when the Spirit is grieved, He withdraws His blessings.

The Holy Spirit is also the attesting Spirit (1 John 4:1–6), giving witness to those who are truly God's children. When a believer is abiding in Christ, the Spirit guides him and warns him of false spirits that would lead him astray.

He is also the authenticating Spirit (1 John 5:6–8), bearing witness to the person and work of Jesus Christ. This witness of the Spirit is mentioned in Romans 8:14–16.

Each member of the triune Godhead is involved in the "love life" of a believer. God the Father commands us to love one another, and God the Son gave His life on the cross, the supreme example of love. And God the Holy Spirit lives within us to provide the love we need (Rom. 5:5). To abide in love is to abide in God, and to abide in God is to abide in love. Christian love is not something we "work up" when we need it. Christian love is "shed abroad in our hearts by the Holy Ghost," and this is your constant experience as you abide in Christ.

There are four levels on which a person may live. He may choose the lowest level—Satan's level—and practice murder. Murderers "have their part in the lake which burneth with fire and brimstone: which is the second death" (Rev. 21:8).

Or, a person may choose the next level—hatred. But hatred, in God's sight, is the same as murder. A man who lives with hatred is slowly killing himself, not the other person! Psychiatrists warn that malice and hatred cause all kinds of physical and emotional problems. In fact, one specialist has titled his book *Love or Perish*!

The third level—indifference—is far better than the first two, because the first two are not Christian at all. A man who has constant hatred in his heart, or who habitually murders, proves he has never been born of God. But it is possible to be a Christian and be indifferent to the needs of others.

A man who murders belongs to the Devil, like Cain. A man who hates belongs to the world, which is under Satan's control. But a Christian who is indifferent is living for the flesh, which serves Satan's purposes.

The only happy, holy way to live is on the highest level, the level of Christian love. This is the life of joy and liberty, the life of answered prayer. It assures you confidence and courage in spite of the difficulties of life.

Dr. Rene Spitz of New York made a study of children in foundling homes to determine what effect love and neglect had on them. The survey proved that children who were neglected and unloved were much slower in their development, and some of them even died. Even in a physical sense, love is the very atmosphere of life and growth.

It is even more so in the spiritual sense.

In fact, it is a matter of love or death!

# QUESTIONS FOR PERSONAL REFLECTION
# OR GROUP DISCUSSION

1. John has three main themes in his letter: love, truth, and obedience. How are obedience and love connected?

2. How are love and the truth about Christ connected?

3. Why is hatred so serious a sin?

4. Why do you think indifference to the needs of others is such a common and dangerous sin, even among Christians?

5. What does John mean when he says we should be willing to "lay down our lives for the brethren"?

6. How does love lead to assurance?

7. "When our delight is in the love of God, our desires will be in the will of God." What does that mean to you?

8. What's it like to have a moment-by-moment communion with Christ? Is this something just for special Christians? Explain.

9. How can you abide in God this week?

# Chapter Eight

# Getting to the Bottom of Love

## (1 John 4:1–16)

For the third time, we are considering the subject of love!

This does not mean John ran out of ideas and had to repeat himself. It means that the Holy Spirit, who inspired John, presents the subject once more, from a deeper point of view.

First, love for the brethren has been shown as proof of fellowship with God (1 John 2:7–11); then it has been presented as proof of sonship (1 John 3:10–14). In the earlier passage, love for the brethren is a matter of light or darkness; in the second it is a matter of life or death.

But in 1 John 4:7–16, we get down to the very foundation of the matter. Here we discover why love is such an important part of the life that is real. Love is a valid test of our fellowship and our sonship because "God is love." Love is part of the very being and nature of God. If we are united to God through faith in Christ, we share His nature. And since His nature is love, love is the test of the reality of our spiritual life.

A navigator depends on a compass to help him determine his course. But why a compass? Because it shows him his directions. And why does the compass point north? Because it is so constituted that it responds to the magnetic field that is part of the earth's makeup. The compass is responsive to the nature of the earth.

So with Christian love. The nature of God is love. And a person who knows God and has been born of God will respond to God's nature. As a compass naturally points north, a believer will naturally practice love because love is the nature of God. This love will not be a forced response; it will be a natural response. A believer's love for the brethren will be proof of his sonship and fellowship.

Three times in this section John encouraged us to love one another (1 John 4:7, 11–12). He supported these admonitions by giving us three foundational facts about God.

## 1. What God Is: "God Is Love" (4:7–8)

This is the third of three expressions in John's writings that help us understand the nature of God: "God is spirit" (John 4:24 NASB); "God is light" (1 John 1:5); and "God is love." None of these is a complete revelation of God, of course, and it is wrong to separate them.

God is spirit as to His essence; He is not flesh and blood. To be sure, Jesus Christ now has a glorified body in heaven, and one day we shall have bodies like His. But being by nature spirit, God is not limited by time and space the way His creatures are.

God is light. This refers to His holy nature. In the Bible, light is a symbol of holiness, and darkness is a symbol of sin (John 3:18–21; 1 John 1:5–10). God cannot sin because He is holy. Because we have been born into His family, we have received His holy nature (1 Peter 1:14–16; 2 Peter 1:4).

God is love. This does not mean that "love is God." And the fact that two people "love each other" does not mean that their love is necessarily holy. It has accurately been said that "love does not define God, but God defines love." God is love and God is light; therefore, His love is a holy love, and His holiness is expressed in love. All that God does expresses all that God is. Even His judgments are measured out in love and mercy (Lam. 3:22–23).

Much that is called "love" in modern society bears no resemblance or relationship to the holy, spiritual love of God. Yet we see banners saying "God is love!" displayed at many festivals, particularly where young people are "doing their own thing"—as if one could dignify immorality by calling it "love."

Christian love is a special kind of love. First John 4:10 may be translated: "In this way is seen the true love." There is a false love, and this kind of love God must reject. Love that is born out of the very essence of God must be spiritual and holy, because "God is spirit" and "God is light." This true love is "poured out within our hearts through the Holy Spirit who was given to us" (Rom. 5:5 NASB).

Love, therefore, is a valid test of true Christian faith. Since God is love, and we have claimed a personal relationship with God, we must of necessity reveal His love in how we live. A child of God has been "born of God," and therefore he shares God's divine nature. Since "God is love," Christians ought to love one another. The logic is unanswerable!

Not only have we been "born of God," but we also "know God." In the Bible, the word *know* has a much deeper meaning than simply intellectual acquaintance or understanding. For example, the verb "know" is used to describe the intimate union of husband and wife (Gen. 4:1). To know God means to be in a deep relationship to Him—to share His life and enjoy His love. This knowing is not simply a matter of understanding facts; it is a matter of perceiving truth (see 1 John 2:3–5).

We must understand "he that loveth not knoweth not God" (1 John 4:8) in this light. Certainly many unsaved people love their families and even sacrifice for them. And no doubt many of these same people have some kind of intellectual understanding of God. What, then, do they lack? They lack a personal experience of God. To paraphrase 1 John 4:8, "The person who does not have this divine kind of love has never entered into a personal, experiential knowledge of God. What he knows is in his head, but it has never gotten into his heart."

What God is determines what we ought to be. "As he is, so are we in this world" (1 John 4:17). The fact that Christians love one another is evidence of their fellowship with God and their sonship from God, and it is also evidence that they know God. Their experience with God is not simply a once-for-all crisis; it is a daily experience of getting to know Him better and better. True theology (the study of God) is not a dry, impractical course in doctrine—it is an exciting day-by-day experience that makes us Christlike!

A large quantity of radioactive material was stolen from a hospital. When the hospital administrator notified the police, he said, "Please warn the thief that he is carrying death with him, and that the radioactive material cannot be successfully hidden. As long as he has it in his possession, it is affecting him disastrously!"

A person who claims he knows God and is in union with Him must be personally affected by this relationship. A Christian ought to become what God is, and "God is love." To argue otherwise is to prove that one does not really know God!

## 2. What God Did: "He Sent His Son" (4:9–11)

Because God is love, He must communicate—not only in words but in deeds. True love is never static or inactive. God reveals His love to mankind in many ways. He has geared all of creation to meeting men's needs. Until man's sin brought creation under bondage, man had on earth a perfect home in which to love and serve God.

God's love was revealed in the way He dealt with the nation of Israel. "The Lord did not set his love upon you, nor choose you, because ye were more in number than any people; for ye were the fewest of all people. But because the LORD loved you … hath the LORD brought you out with a mighty hand" (Deut. 7:7–8).

The greatest expression of God's love is in the death of His Son. "But God demonstrates His own love toward us, in that while we were yet sinners, Christ died for us" (Rom. 5:8 NASB).

The word *manifested* means "to come out in the open, to be made public." It is the opposite of "to hide, to make secret." Under the old covenant, God was hidden behind the shadows of ritual and ceremony (Heb. 10:1); but in Jesus Christ "the life was manifested" (1 John 1:2). "He that hath seen me," said Jesus, "hath seen the Father" (John 14:9).

Why was Jesus Christ manifested? "And you know that he was manifested to take away our sins" (1 John 3:5). "For this purpose the Son of God was manifested, that he might destroy the works of the devil" (v. 8). Where did Jesus take away our sins and destroy (render inoperative) the works of the Devil? At the cross! God manifested His love at the cross when He gave His Son as a sacrifice there for our sins.

This is the only place in the epistle where Jesus is called God's only begotten Son. The title is used in John's gospel (John 1:14). It means "unique, the only one of its kind." The fact that God sent His Son into the world is one evidence of the deity of Jesus Christ. Babies are not sent into the world from some other place; they are born into the world. As the perfect Man, Jesus was born into the world, but as the eternal Son, He was sent into the world.

But the sending of Christ into the world and His death on the cross were not prompted by man's love for God. They were prompted by His love for man. The world's attitude toward God is anything but love!

Two purposes are given for Christ's death on the cross: that we might live through Him (1 John 4:9) and that He might be the propitiation for our sins (v. 10). His death was not an accident; it was an appointment. He did not die as a weak martyr, but as a mighty conqueror.

Jesus Christ died that we might live "through him" (1 John 4:9), "for him" (2 Cor. 5:15 NASB), and "with him" (1 Thess. 5:9–10). A sinner's desperate need is for life, because he is "dead in trespasses and sins" (Eph. 2:1). It is something of a paradox that Christ had to die so that we may live! We can never probe the mystery of His death, but this we know: He died for us (Gal. 2:20).

The death of Christ is described as a "propitiation." John has used this word before (1 John 2:2), so there is no need to study it in detail again. We should remember that propitiation does not mean that men must do something to appease God or to placate His anger. Propitiation is something God does to make it possible for men to be forgiven. "God is light," and therefore He must uphold His holy law. "God is love," and therefore He wants to forgive and save sinners. How can God forgive sinners and still be consistent with His holy nature? The answer is the cross. There Jesus Christ bore the punishment for sin and met the just demands of the holy law. But there, also, God reveals His love and makes it possible for men to be saved by faith.

It is important to note that the emphasis is on the death of Christ, not on His birth. The fact that Jesus was "made flesh" (John 1:14) is certainly an evidence of God's grace and love, but the fact that He was "made sin" (2 Cor. 5:21) is underscored for us. The example of Christ, the teachings of Christ, the whole earthly life of Christ, find their true meaning and fulfillment in the cross.

For the second time, believers are exhorted to "love one another" (1 John 4:11). This exhortation is a commandment to be obeyed (v. 7), and its basis is the nature of God. "God is love; we know God; therefore, we should love one another." But the exhortation to love one another is presented as a privilege as well as a responsibility: "If God so loved us, we ought also to love one another" (v. 11). We are not saved by loving Christ; we are saved by believing on Christ (John 3:16). But after we realize what

He did for us on the cross, our normal response ought to be to love Him and to love one another.

It is important that Christians progress in their understanding of love. To love one another simply out of a sense of duty is good, but to love out of appreciation (rather than obligation) is even better.

This may be one reason why Jesus established the Lord's Supper, the Communion service. When we break the bread and share the cup, we remember His death. Few men, if any, want their deaths remembered! In fact, we remember the life of a loved one and try to forget the sadness of his death. Not so with Christ. He commands us to remember His death: "This do in remembrance of me"!

We should remember our Lord's death in a spiritual way, not merely sentimentally. Someone has defined sentiment as "feeling without responsibility." It is easy to experience solemn emotions at a church service and yet go out to live the same defeated life. True spiritual experience involves the whole man. The mind must understand spiritual truth; the heart must love and appreciate it, and the will must act on it. The deeper we go into the meaning of the cross, the greater will be our love for Christ and the greater our active concern for one another.

We have discovered what God is and what God has done, but a third foundation fact takes us even deeper into the meaning and implications of Christian love.

### 3. WHAT GOD IS DOING: "GOD ABIDES IN US" (4:12–16)

At this point it would be good for us to review what John has been saying about the basic truth that "God is love."

This truth is revealed to us in the Word, but it was also revealed on the cross, where Christ died for us. "God is love" is not simply a doctrine in the Bible; it is an eternal fact clearly demonstrated at Calvary. God has said something to us, and God has done something for us.

But all this is preparation for the third great fact: God does something in us! We are not merely students reading a book, or spectators watching a deeply moving event. We are participants in the great drama of God's love!

In order to save money, a college drama class purchased only a few scripts of a play and cut them up into the separate parts. The director gave each player his individual part in order and then started to rehearse the play. But nothing went right. After an hour of missed cues and mangled sequences, the cast gave up.

At that point, the director sat the actors all on the stage and said: "Look, I'm going to read the entire play to you, so don't any of you say a word." He read the entire script aloud, and when he was finished, one of the actors said: "So that's what it was all about!"

And when they understood the entire story, they were able to fit their parts together and have a successful rehearsal.

When you read 1 John 4:12–16, you feel like saying, "So that's what it's all about!" Because here we discover what God had in mind when He devised His great plan of salvation.

To begin with, God's desire is to live in us. He is not satisfied simply to tell us that He loves us, or even show us that He loves us.

It is interesting to trace God's dwelling places as recorded in the Bible. In the beginning, God had fellowship with man in a personal, direct way (Gen. 3:8), but sin broke that fellowship. It was necessary for God to shed the blood of animals to cover the sins of Adam and Eve so that they might come back into His fellowship.

One of the key words in the book of Genesis is walked. God *walked* with men, and men walked with God. Enoch (Gen. 5:22), Noah (6:9), and Abram (Abraham) walked with God (17:1; 24:40).

But by the time of the events recorded in Exodus, a change had taken place: God did not simply walk with men, He lived, or dwelt, with them.

God's commandment to Israel was "And let them make me a sanctuary; that I may dwell among them" (Ex. 25:8). The first of those sanctuaries was the tabernacle. When Moses dedicated it, the glory of God came down and moved into the tent (40:33–35).

God dwelt in the camp, but He did not dwell in the bodies of the individual Israelites.

Unfortunately, the nation sinned and God's glory departed (1 Sam. 4:21). But God used Samuel and David to restore the nation, and Solomon built God a magnificent temple. When the temple was dedicated, once again the glory of God came to dwell in the land (1 Kings 8:1–11).

But history repeated itself, and Israel disobeyed God and was taken into captivity. The gorgeous temple was destroyed. One of the prophets of the captivity, Ezekiel, saw the glory of God depart from it (Ezek. 8:4; 9:3; 10:4; 11:22–23).

Did the glory ever return? Yes—in the Person of God's Son, Jesus Christ! "And the Word became flesh, and tabernacled among us, and we beheld His glory" (John 1:14, literal translation). The glory of God dwelt on earth in the body of Jesus Christ, for His body was the temple of God (John 2:18–22). But wicked men nailed His body to a cross. They crucified "the Lord of glory" (1 Cor. 2:8). All this was part of God's thrilling plan, and Christ arose from the dead, returned to heaven, and sent His Holy Spirit to dwell in men.

The glory of God now lives in the bodies of God's children. "Or do you not know that your body is a temple of the Holy Spirit who is in you, whom you have from God, and that you are not your own?" (1 Cor. 6:19 NASB). The glory of God departed from the tabernacle and the temple when Israel disobeyed God, but Jesus has promised that the Spirit will abide in us forever (John 14:16).

With this background, we can better understand what 1 John 4:12–16 is saying to us. God is invisible (1 Tim. 1:17), and no man can see Him in His essence. Jesus is "the image of the invisible God" (Col. 1:15). By taking on Himself a human body, Jesus was able to reveal God to us. But Jesus is no longer here on earth. How, then, does God reveal Himself to the world?

He reveals Himself through the lives of His children. Men cannot see God, but they can see us. If we abide in Christ, we will love one another, and our love for one another will reveal God's love to a needy world. God's love will be experienced in us and then will be expressed through us.

That important little word *abide* (or "dwell") is used six times in 1 John 4:12–16. It refers to our personal fellowship with Jesus Christ. To abide in Christ means to remain in spiritual oneness with Him, so that no sin comes between us. Because we are "born of God," we have union with Christ, but it is only as we trust Him and obey His commandments that we have communion with Him. Much as a faithful husband and wife "abide in love" though they may be separated by miles, so a believer abides in God's love. This abiding is made possible by the indwelling of the Holy Spirit (1 John 4:13).

Imagine the wonder and the privilege of having God abide in you! The Old Testament Israelite would look with wonder at the tabernacle or temple because the presence of God was in that building. No man would dare to enter the Holy of Holies, where God was enthroned in glory! But we have God's Spirit living in us! We abide in this love, and we experience the abiding of God in us. "If a man love me, he will keep my words: and my Father will love him, and we will come unto him, and make our abode with him" (John 14:23).

God's love is proclaimed in the Word ("God is love") and proved at the cross. But here we have something deeper: God's love is perfected in the believer. Fantastic as it may seem, God's love is not made perfect in angels, but in sinners saved by His grace. We Christians are now the tabernacles and temples in which God dwells. He reveals His love through us.

Dr. G. Campbell Morgan, famous British preacher, had five sons, all of whom became ministers of the gospel. One day a visitor in their home dared to ask a personal question: "Which of you six is the best preacher?"

Their united answer was "Mother!"

Of course, Mrs. Morgan had never preached a formal sermon in a church, but her life was a constant sermon on the love of God. The life of a Christian who abides in God's love is a potent witness for God in the world. Men cannot see God, but they can see His love moving us to deeds of helpfulness and kindness.

Three different witnesses are suggested in these verses: (1) The witness of the believer that Jesus Christ is God's Son (1 John 4:15); (2) the witness in the believer by the Spirit (v. 13); and (3) the witness through the believer that God is love and that He sent His Son to die for the world (v. 14).

These witnesses cannot be separated. The world will not believe that God loves sinners until they see His love at work in His children's lives.

A Salvation Army worker found a derelict woman alone on the street and invited her to come into the chapel for help, but the woman refused to move. The worker assured her, "We love you and want to help you. God loves you. Jesus died for you." But the woman did not budge.

As if on divine impulse, the Army lassie leaned over and kissed the woman on the cheek, taking her into her arms. The woman began to sob and, like a child, was led into the chapel, where she ultimately trusted Christ.

"You told me that God loved me," she said later, "but it wasn't till you showed me that God loved me that I wanted to be saved."

Jesus did not simply preach the love of God; He proved it by giving His life on the cross. He expects His followers to do likewise. If we abide in Christ, we will abide in His love. If we abide in His love, we must share this love with others. Whenever we share this love, it is proof in our own hearts that we are abiding in Christ. In other words, there is no separation between a Christian's inner life and his outer life.

Abiding in God's love produces two wonderful spiritual benefits in the life of a believer: (1) he grows in knowledge, and (2) he grows in faith. The more we love God, the more we understand the love of God. And the more we understand His love, the easier it is for us to trust Him. After all, when you know someone intimately and love him sincerely, you have no problem putting your confidence in him.

A man standing in the greeting card section of a store was having trouble picking out a card. The clerk asked if she could help, and he said, "Well, it's our fortieth wedding anniversary, but I can't find a card that says what I want to say. You know, forty years ago it wouldn't have been any problem picking out a card, because back then I thought I knew what love was. But we love each other so much more today, I just can't find a card that says it!"

This is a growing Christian's experience with God. As he abides in Christ and spends time in fellowship with Him, he comes to love God more and more. He also grows in his love for other Christians, for the lost, and even for his enemies. As he shares the Father's love with others, he experiences more of the Father's love himself. He understands the Father's love better and better.

"God is love," then, is not simply a profound biblical statement. It is the basis for a believer's relationship with God and with his fellow man. Because God is love, we can love. His love is not past history; it is present reality. "Love one another" begins as a commandment (1 John 4:7), then it becomes a privilege (v. 11). But it is more than a commandment or a privilege. It is also the thrilling consequence and evidence of our abiding in Christ (v. 12). Loving one another is not something we simply ought to do; it is something we want to do.

Some practical applications grow out of this basic truth:

First, the better we know God's love, the easier it will be to live as a Christian. Bible knowledge alone does not take the place of personal experience of God's love. In fact, it can be a dangerous substitute if we are not careful.

Helen came home from a youth retreat greatly enthused over what she had learned.

"We had some terrific sessions on how to have personal devotions," she told her sister Joyce. "I plan to have my devotions every single day."

A week later, while Joyce was running the vacuum cleaner, she heard Helen screaming, "Do you have to make all that noise? Don't you know I'm trying to have my devotions?" And the verbal explosion was followed by the slamming of a door.

Helen still had to learn that personal devotions are not an end in themselves. If they do not help us love God and love one another, they are accomplishing little. The Bible is a revelation of God's love, and the better we understand His love, the easier it should be for us to obey Him and love others.

A second consideration is that unless we love the lost, our verbal witness to them will be useless. The gospel message is a message of love. This love was both declared and demonstrated by Jesus Christ. The only way we can effectively win others is to declare the gospel and demonstrate it in how we live. Too much "witnessing" today is a mere mouthing of words. People need an expression of love.

One reason why God permits the world to hate Christians is so that Christians may return love for the world's hatred. "Blessed are you when people insult you and persecute you, and falsely say all kinds of evil against you because of Me…. But I say to you, love your enemies and pray for those who persecute you" (Matt. 5:11, 44 NASB).

"Pastor, the Bible tells us to love our neighbors, but I doubt that anybody could love my neighbors," Mrs. Barton said at the close of a Sunday school lesson. "I've tried to be nice to them, but it just doesn't work."

"Perhaps 'being nice to them' isn't the real answer," the pastor explained. "You know, it's possible to be nice to people with the wrong motive."

"You mean as though you're trying to buy them off?"

"Something like that. I think you and I had better pray that God will give you a true spiritual love for your neighbors. If you love them in a Christian way, you'll not be able to do them any damage," the pastor pointed out.

It took some weeks, but Mrs. Barton grew in her love for her neighbors, and she also found herself growing in her own spiritual life.

"My neighbors haven't changed a whole lot," she told the prayer group, "but my attitude toward them has really changed. I used to do things for them to try to win their approval. But now I do things for Jesus' sake, because He died for them—and it makes all the difference in the world!"

In this paragraph of his letter, John has taken us to the very foundation of Christian love. But he still had more to teach us. In the next section, he deals with our own personal love for God and how God perfects that love in us.

These two aspects of Christian love cannot be separated from one another: If we love God, we will love one another; and if we love one another, we will grow in our love for God.

And both statements are true because "God is love."

# QUESTIONS FOR PERSONAL REFLECTION OR GROUP DISCUSSION

1. What common misinterpretations are made of the biblical teaching that God is love?

2. What does "God is love" really mean?

3. What are some ways God has revealed His love to people?

4. According to 1 John 4:9, one reason why God sent His Son is so that we might live through Him. What does it mean to live through Christ?

5. What motivations for loving other people do you find in 4:7–16?

6. What does it mean to abide/dwell/live in Christ, as 4:12–16 describes? How do we go about doing that?

7. Since Jesus is no longer on earth, how does God reveal Himself to the world? What implications does this have for you?

8. If we love one another, God's love is made "complete" or "perfect" in us (4:12). How do you respond to that idea that God's love can be made complete in you?

9. "There is no separation between a Christian's inner life and his outer life." What does that mean in our practical, everyday living?

10. How has God's love been demonstrated to you recently through another Christian?

# Chapter Nine

# LOVE, HONOR, AND OBEY

## (1 John 4:17—5:5)

The prospective bridegroom was extremely nervous as he and his fiancée were discussing their wedding plans with their pastor.

"I'd like to see a copy of the wedding vows," the young man said, and the pastor handed him the service. He read it carefully, handed it back, and said, "That won't do! There's nothing written in there about her obeying me!"

His fiancée smiled, took his hand, and said, "Honey, the word *obey* doesn't have to be written in a book. It's already written in love in my heart."

This is the truth in view in this portion of 1 John. Up to this point, the emphasis has been on Christians loving one another; but now we turn to a deeper—and more important—topic: a believer's love for the Father. We cannot love our neighbors or our brothers unless we love our heavenly Father. We must first love God with all our hearts; then we can love our neighbors as ourselves.

The key word in this section is *perfect*. God wants to perfect in us His love for us and our love for Him. The word *perfect* carries the idea of maturity and completeness. A believer is not only to grow in grace and knowledge (2 Peter 3:18), but he is also to grow in his love for the Father. He does this in response to the Father's love for him.

How much does God love us? Enough to send His Son to die for us (John 3:16). He loves His children in the same way as He loves Christ (17:23). And Jesus tells us that the Father wants the love with which He loved the Son to be in His children (17:26).

In other words, the Christian life is to be a daily experience of growing in the love of God. It involves a Christian's coming to know his heavenly Father in a much deeper way as he grows in love.

It is easy to fragment the Christian life and become preoccupied with individual pieces instead of the total picture. One group may emphasize "holiness" and urge its members to get victory over sin. Another may stress "witnessing" or "separation from the world." But each of these emphases is really a by-product of something else: a believer's growing love for the Father. Mature Christian love is the great universal need among God's people.

How can a believer know that his love for the Father is being perfected? This paragraph of 1 John suggests four evidences.

## 1. CONFIDENCE (4:17–19)

Two brand-new words came into John's vocabulary here: fear and torment. And this is written to believers! Is it possible that Christians can actually live in fear and torment? Yes, unfortunately, many professed believers experience both fear and torment day after day. And the reason is that they are not growing in the love of God.

The word *boldness* can mean "confidence" or "freedom of speech." It does not mean brazenness or brashness. A believer who experiences perfecting love grows in his confidence toward God. He has a reverential fear of God, not a tormenting fear. He is a son who respects his Father, not a prisoner who cringes before a judge.

We have adopted the Greek word for fear into our English vocabulary:

phobia. All sorts of phobias are listed in psychology books; for instance, acrophobia—"fear of heights"—and hydrophobia—"fear of water." John was writing about krisisphobia—"fear of judgment." John has already mentioned this solemn truth in 1 John 2:28, and now he deals with it again.

If people are afraid, it is because of something in the past that haunts them, or something in the present that upsets them, or something in the future that they feel threatens them. Or it may be a combination of all three. A believer in Jesus Christ does not have to fear the past, present, or future, for he has experienced the love of God, and this love is being perfected in him day by day.

"It is appointed unto men once to die, but after this the judgment" (Heb. 9:27). But a Christian does not fear future judgment because Christ has suffered his judgment for him on the cross. "Truly, truly I say to you, he who hears My word, and believes Him who sent Me, has eternal life, and does not come into judgment, but has passed out of death into life" (John 5:24 NASB). "Therefore there is now no condemnation for those who are in Christ Jesus" (Rom. 8:1 NASB). For a Christian, judgment is not future; it is past. His sins have been judged already at the cross, and they will never be brought against him again.

The secret of our boldness is "As he is, so are we in this world" (1 John 4:17). We know that "we shall be like him" when He returns (3:1–2), but that statement refers primarily to the glorified bodies believers will receive (Phil. 3:20–21). Positionally, we are right now "as he is." We are so closely identified with Christ, as members of His body, that our position in this world is like His exalted position in heaven.

This means that the Father deals with us as He deals with His own beloved Son. How, then, can we ever be afraid?

We do not have to be afraid of the future because our sins were judged in Christ when He died on the cross. The Father cannot judge our sins again without judging His Son, for "as He is, so are we in this world."

We do not have to be afraid of the past, because "He first loved us." From the very first, our relationship to God was one of love. It was not that we loved Him, but that He loved us (see 1 John 4:10). "For if while we were enemies we were reconciled to God through the death of His Son, much more, having been reconciled, we shall be saved by His life" (Rom. 5:10 NASB). If God loved us when we were outside the family, disobeying Him, how much more does He love us now that we are His children!

We do not need to fear the present because "perfect love casteth out fear" (1 John 4:18). As we grow in the love of God, we cease to be fearful of what He will do.

Of course there is a proper "fear of God," but it is not the kind of fear that produces torment. "For you have not received a spirit of slavery leading to fear again, but you have received a spirit of adoption as sons by which we cry out, 'Abba! Father!'" (Rom. 8:15 NASB). "For God hath not given us a spirit of fear; but of power, and of love, and of a sound mind" (2 Tim. 1:7).

Fear is actually the beginning of torment. We torment ourselves as we contemplate what lies ahead. Many people suffer acutely when they contemplate a visit to the dentist. Think of how an unsaved person must suffer as he contemplates the day of judgment. But since a Christian has boldness in the day of judgment, he can have boldness as he faces life today, for there is no situation of life today that begins to compare with the terrible severity of the day of judgment.

God wants His children to live in an atmosphere of love and confidence, not fear and torment. We need not fear life or death, for we are being perfected in the love of God. "Who will separate us from the love of Christ? Will tribulation, or distress, or persecution, or famine, or nakedness, or peril, or sword? … But in all these things we overwhelmingly conquer through Him who loved us. For I am convinced that neither death, nor life, nor angels, nor principalities, nor things present, nor things to come, nor powers, nor height, nor depth, nor any other created thing, will be able to separate us from the love of God, which is in Christ Jesus our Lord" (Rom. 8:35, 37–39 NASB).

Imagine! Nothing in all creation—present or future—can come between us and God's love!

The perfecting of God's love in our lives is usually a matter of several stages. When we were lost, we lived in fear and knew nothing of God's love. After we trusted Christ, we found a perplexing mixture of both fear and love in our hearts. But as we grew in fellowship with the Father, gradually the fear vanished, and our hearts were controlled by His love alone. An immature Christian is tossed between fear and love; a mature Christian rests in God's love.

A growing confidence in the presence of God is one of the first evidences that our love for God is maturing. But confidence never stands alone; it always leads to other moral results.

## 2. HONESTY (4:20–21)

Here it is for the seventh time: "If a man say …"!

We have met this important phrase several times, and each time we knew what was coming: a warning against pretending.

Fear and pretense usually go together. In fact, they were born together when the first man and woman sinned. No sooner did Adam and Eve sense their guilt than they tried to hide from God and cover their nakedness. But neither their coverings nor their excuses could shelter them from God's all-seeing eye. Adam finally had to admit, "I heard thy voice in the garden, and I was afraid" (Gen. 3:10).

But when our hearts are confident toward God, there is no need for us to pretend, either to God or to other people. A Christian who lacks confidence with God will also lack confidence with God's people. Part of the torment that fear generates is the constant worry, "How much do others really know about me?" But when we have confidence with God, this fear is gone, and we can face both God and men without worry.

"How many members do you have in your church?" a visitor asked the pastor.

"Somewhere near a thousand," the pastor replied.

"That certainly is a lot of people to try to please!" the visitor exclaimed.

"Let me assure you, my friend, that I have never tried to please all my members, or even some of them," the pastor said with a smile. "I aim to please one Person—the Lord Jesus Christ. If I am right with Him, then everything should be right between me and my people."

An immature Christian who is not growing in his love for God may think he has to impress others with his "spirituality." This mistake turns him into a liar! He is professing something that he is not really practicing; he is playing a role instead of living a life.

Perhaps the best example of this sin is seen in the experience of Ananias and Sapphira (Acts 5). They sold a piece of property and brought part of the money to the Lord, but they gave the impression that they were bringing all the money. The sin of this couple was not in taking money from God, for Peter made it clear that the disposal of the money was up to them (v. 4). Their sin was hypocrisy. They were trying to make people think they were more generous and spiritual than they really were.

Pretending is one of the favorite activities of little children, but it is certainly not a mark of maturity in adults. Adults must know themselves and be themselves, fulfilling the purposes for which Christ saved them. Their lives must be marked by honesty.

Spiritual honesty brings peace and power to the person who practices it. He does not have to keep a record of the lies he has told, and he is not using his energy to cover up. Because he lives in open honesty with the Father, he can live in honesty with other people. Love and truth go together. Because he knows God loves him and accepts him (even with all his faults), he is not trying to impress others. He loves God, and therefore he loves his fellow Christians.

Jerry's grades were far below his usual performance, and on top of that, his health seemed to be failing. His new roommate was concerned about him and finally persuaded him to talk to the campus psychologist.

"I can't figure myself out," Jerry admitted. "Last year I was sailing through school, and this year it is like fighting a war."

"You're not having trouble with your new roommate, are you?" the counselor asked.

Jerry did not reply right away, and this gave the counselor a clue.

"Jerry, are you concentrating on living your life as a good student, or on trying to impress your new roommate with your abilities?"

"Yeah, I guess that's it," Jerry answered with a sigh of relief. "I've worn myself out acting and haven't had enough energy left for living."

Confidence toward God and honesty with others are two marks of maturity that are bound to show up when our love for God is being perfected.

## 3. Joyful Obedience (5:1–3)

Not simply obedience—but joyful obedience! "His commandments are not burdensome" (1 John 5:3 NASB).

Everything in creation—except man—obeys the will of God. "Fire, and hail; snow, and vapor; stormy wind fulfilling his word" (Ps. 148:8). In the book of Jonah, you see the winds and waves, and even the fish, obeying God's commands, but the prophet persisted in disobeying. Even a plant and a little worm did what God commanded. But the prophet stubbornly wanted his own way.

Disobedience to God's will is a tragedy—but so is reluctant, grudging obedience. God does not want us to disobey Him, but neither does He want us to obey out of fear or necessity. What Paul wrote about giving also applies to living: "not grudgingly or under compulsion, for God loves a cheerful giver" (2 Cor. 9:7 NASB).

What is the secret of joyful obedience? It is to recognize that obedience is a family matter. We are serving a loving Father and helping our brothers and sisters in Christ. We have been born of God, we love God, and we love God's children. And we demonstrate this love by keeping God's commandments.

A woman visited a newspaper editor's office, hoping to sell him some poems she had written.

"What are your poems about?" the editor asked.

"They're about love!" gushed the poetess.

The editor settled back in his chair and said, "Well, read me a poem. The world could certainly use a lot more love!"

The poem she read was filled with moons and Junes and other sticky sentiments, and it was more than the editor could take.

"I'm sorry," he said, "but you just don't know what love is all about! It's not moonlight and roses. It's sitting up all night at a sickbed, or working extra hours so the kids can have new shoes. The world doesn't need your brand of poetical love. It needs some good old-fashioned practical love."

D. L. Moody often said, "Every Bible should be bound in shoe leather." We show our love to God not by empty words but by willing works. We are not slaves obeying a master; we are children obeying a Father. And our sin is a family affair.

One of the tests of maturing love is our personal attitude toward the Bible, because in the Bible we find God's will for our lives revealed. An unsaved man considers the Bible an impossible book, mainly because he does not understand its spiritual message (1 Cor. 2:14). An immature Christian considers the demands of the Bible to be burdensome. He is somewhat like a little child who is learning to obey, and who asks, "Why do I have to do that?" or "Wouldn't it be better to do this?"

But a Christian who experiences God's perfecting love finds himself enjoying the Word of God and truly loving it. He does not read the Bible as a textbook, but as a love letter.

The longest chapter in the Bible is Psalm 119, and its theme is the Word of God. Every verse but two (Ps. 119:122, 132) mentions the Word of God in one form or another, as "law," "precepts," "commandments," and so forth. But the interesting thing is that the psalmist loves the Word of God and enjoys telling us about it! "O how love I thy law!" (v. 97). He rejoices in the law (vv. 14, 162) and delights in it (vv. 16, 24). It is honey to his taste (v. 103). In fact, he turns God's law into a song: "Thy statutes have been my songs in the house of my pilgrimage" (v. 54).

Imagine turning statutes into songs. Suppose the local symphony presented a concert of the traffic code set to music! Most of us do not consider laws a source of joyful song, but this is the way the psalmist looked at God's law. Because he loved the Lord, he loved His law. God's commandments were not grievous and burdensome to him. Just as a loving son or daughter happily obeys his father's command, so a Christian with perfecting love joyfully obeys God's command.

At this point, we can review and understand the practical meaning of "maturing love" in our daily lives. As our love for the Father matures, we have confidence and are no longer afraid of His will. We also are honest toward others and lose our fear of being rejected. And we have a new attitude toward the Word of God: It is the expression of God's love, and we enjoy obeying it. Confidence toward God, honesty toward others, and joyful obedience are the marks of perfecting love and the ingredients that make up a happy Christian life.

We can see, too, how sin ruins all this. When we disobey God we lose our confidence toward Him. If we do not immediately confess our sin and claim His forgiveness (1 John 1:9), we must start pretending in order to cover up. Disobedience leads to dishonesty, and both turn our hearts away from the Word of God. Instead of reading the Word with joy to discover the Father's will, we ignore the Word or perhaps read it in a routine way.

The burden of religion (man trying to please God in his own strength) is a grievous one (see Matt. 23:4), but the yoke that Christ puts on us is not burdensome at all (11:28–30). Love lightens burdens. Jacob had to work for seven years to win the woman he loved, but the Bible tells us that "they seemed unto him a few days, for the love he had to her" (Gen. 29:20). Perfecting love produces joyful obedience.

## 4. Victory (5:4–5)

The Greek goddess of victory was Nike, which also happens to be the name of a United States aerial missile. Both of them are named for the Greek word *nike* (NEE-kay), which simply means "victory." But what does victory have to do with maturing love?

Christians live in a real world and are beset with formidable obstacles. It is not easy to obey God. It is much easier to drift with the world, disobey Him, and "do your own thing."

But the Christian is "born of God." This means he has the divine nature within him, and it is impossible for this divine nature to disobey God. "For whatever is born of God overcomes the world" (1 John 5:4 NASB). If the old nature is in control of us, we disobey God, but if the new nature is in control, we obey God. The world appeals to the old nature (2:15–17) and tries to make God's commandments seem burdensome.

Our victory is a result of faith, and we grow in faith as we grow in love. The more you love someone, the easier it is to trust him. The more our love for Christ is perfected, the more our faith in Christ is perfected too, because faith and love mature together.

The word *overcome* was a favorite with John; he used it in 1 John 2:13–14 with reference to overcoming the Devil. He used it seven times in Revelation to describe believers and the blessings they receive (Rev. 2:7,

11, 17, 26; 3:5, 12, 21). He was not describing a special class of believers. Rather, he was using the word *overcomer* as a name for the true Christian. Because we have been born of God, we are overcomers.

We are told that a soldier in the army of Alexander the Great was not acting bravely in battle. When he should have been pressing ahead, he was lingering behind.

The great general approached him and asked, "What is your name, soldier?"

The man replied, "My name, sir, is Alexander."

The general looked him straight in the eye and said firmly, "Soldier, get in there and fight—or change your name!"

What is our name? "Children of God—the born-again ones of God." Alexander the Great wanted his name to be a symbol of courage; our name carries with it assurance of victory. To be born of God means to share God's victory.

This is a victory of faith, but faith in what? Faith in Jesus Christ, the Son of God! The person who overcomes the world is the one "who believes that Jesus is the Son of God" (1 John 5:5 NASB). It is not faith in ourselves, but faith in Christ, that gives us the victory. "In the world ye shall have tribulation but be of good cheer; I have overcome the world" (John 16:33).

Identification with Christ in His victory reminds us of the several times we have read "as he is" in John's letter. "As he is, so are we in this world" (1 John 4:17). We should walk in the light "as he is in the light" (1:7). If we claim to abide in Him, then we should conduct ourselves as He conducted Himself (2:6). His children are to be on earth what He is in heaven. It is only necessary for us to claim this wonderful position by faith—and to act on it.

When Jesus Christ died, we died with Him. Paul said, "I have been crucified with Christ" (Gal. 2:20 NASB). When Christ was buried, we were buried with Him. And when He arose, we arose with Him. "Therefore we have been buried with Him through baptism into death, so that as Christ was raised from the dead through the glory of the Father, so we too might walk in newness of life" (Rom. 6:4 NASB).

When Christ ascended to heaven, we ascended with Him and are now seated with Him in heavenly places (Eph. 2:6). And when Christ returns, we shall share His exaltation. "When Christ, who is our life, is revealed, then you also will be revealed with Him in glory" (Col. 3:4 NASB).

All these verses describe our spiritual position in Christ. When we claim this position by faith, we share His victory. When God raised Jesus from the dead, He "seated Him at His right hand in the heavenly places, far above all rule and authority and power and dominion, and every name that is named.… And He put all things in subjection under His feet" (Eph. 1:20–22 NASB). This means that, positionally, each child of God is privileged to sit far above all his enemies!

Where a man sits determines how much authority he may exercise. The man who sits in the general manager's chair has a restricted sphere of authority; the man who sits in the vice president's chair exercises more control. But the man behind the desk marked "president" exercises the most authority. No matter where he may be in the factory or office, he is respected and obeyed because of where he sits. His power is determined by his position, not by his personal appearance or the way he feels.

So with a child of God: His authority is determined by his position in Christ. When he trusted Christ, he was identified with Him by the Holy Spirit and made a member of His body (1 Cor. 12:12–13). His old life has been buried, and he has been raised to a new life of glory. In Christ, he is sitting on the very throne of the universe!

A Civil War veteran used to wander from place to place, begging a bed and bite to eat and always talking about his friend "Mr. Lincoln." Because of his injuries, he was unable to hold a steady job. But as long as he could keep going, he would chat about his beloved president.

"You say you knew Mr. Lincoln," a skeptical bystander retorted one day. "I'm not so sure you did. Prove it!"

The old man replied, "Why, sure, I can prove it. In fact, I have a piece of paper here that Mr. Lincoln himself signed and gave to me."

From his old wallet, the man took out a much-folded piece of paper and showed it to the man.

"I'm not much for reading," he apologized, "but I know that's Mr. Lincoln's signature."

"Man, do you know what you have here?" one of the spectators asked. "You have a generous federal pension authorized by President Lincoln. You don't have to walk around like a poor beggar! Mr. Lincoln has made you rich!"

To paraphrase what John wrote, "You Christians do not have to walk around defeated, because Jesus Christ has made you victors! He has defeated every enemy, and you share His victory. Now, by faith, claim His victory."

The key, of course, is faith, but this has always been God's key to victory. The great men and women named in Hebrews 11 all won their victories "by faith." They simply took God at His word and acted on it, and He honored their faith and gave them victory. Faith is not simply saying that what God says is true; true faith is acting on what God says because it is true. Someone has said that faith is not so much believing in spite of evidence, but obeying in spite of consequence.

Victorious faith is the result of maturing love. The better we come to know and love Jesus Christ, the easier it is to trust Him with the needs and battles of life. It is important that this maturing love become a regular and a practical thing in our daily lives.

How does a believer go about experiencing this kind of love and the blessings that flow from it?

To begin with, this kind of love must be cultivated. It is not the result of a hit-or-miss friendship! A previous study pointed out that a believer slips back into the world by stages:

1. Friendship with the world (James 4:4)
2. Spotted by the world (James 1:27)
3. Loving the world (1 John 2:15–17)
4. Conformed to the world (Rom. 12:2)

Our relationship to Jesus Christ, in a similar way, grows by stages.

**We must cultivate friendship with Christ.** Abraham was "the Friend of God" (James 2:23) because he separated himself from the world and did what God told him. His life was not perfect, but when he sinned, he confessed and went right back to walking with God.

**This friendship will begin to influence our lives.** As we read the Word and pray, and as we fellowship with God's people, Christian graces will start to show up in us. Our thoughts will be cleaner, our conversation more meaningful, our desires more wholesome. But we will not be suddenly and totally changed; it will be a gradual process.

**Our friendship with Christ and our becoming like Him will lead to a deeper love for Christ.** On the human level, friendship often leads to love. On the divine level, friendship with Christ ought to lead to love. "We love Him because He first loved us" (1 John 4:19). The Word of God reveals His love to us, and the indwelling Spirit of God makes this love more and more real to us. Furthermore, this love is worked out in our lives in daily obedience. Christian love is not a passing emotion; it is a permanent devotion, a deep desire to please Christ and to do His will.

**The more we know Him the better we love Him, and the better we love Him the more we become like Him—"*conformed* to the image of His Son" (Rom. 8:29).** Of course we will not be completely conformed to Christ until we see Him (1 John 3:1–3), but we are to begin the process now.

What an exciting way to live! As God's love is perfected in us, we have confidence toward Him and do not live in fear. Because fear is cast out, we can be honest and open; there is no need to pretend. And because fear is gone, our obedience to His commands is born out of love, not terror. We discover that His commandments are not burdensome. Finally, living in this atmosphere of love, honesty, and joyful obedience, we are able to face the world with victorious faith and to overcome instead of being overcome.

The place to begin is not in some daring, dramatic experience. The place to begin is in the quiet, personal place of prayer. Peter wanted to give his life for Jesus, but when he was asked to pray, Peter went to sleep (Luke 22:31–33, 39–46). A believer who begins the day reading the Word, meditating on it, and worshipping Christ in prayer and praise will experience this perfecting love.

When it begins, he will know it—and others will know it. His life will be marked by confidence, honesty, joyful obedience, and victory.

# QUESTIONS FOR PERSONAL REFLECTION
# OR GROUP DISCUSSION

1. What is the meaning of "perfect" love (1 John 4:18)?

2. Why does a Christian need not fear anything—past, present, or future?

3. How does Romans 8:35, 37–39 make you a stronger Christian?

4. In light of what John says in 1 John 4:20–21, why is pretense unnecessary for a Christian?

5. How can 5:1–3 motivate you to joyful obedience?

6. D. L. Moody said, "Every Bible should be bound in shoe leather." What do you think he meant?

7. What does it take to overcome the world (5:4)? Give an example.

8. John emphasizes the importance of believing specific things about Jesus. How are true beliefs linked to love and obedience?

9. "Christian love is not a passing emotion; it is a permanent devotion." Do you agree? Explain.

10. Which of these do you most need to focus on this week: confidence, honesty, joyful obedience, or overcoming the world?

# Chapter Ten

# WHAT DO YOU KNOW FOR SURE?

## (1 John 5:6–21)

Nothing is certain but death and taxes." Benjamin Franklin wrote those words in 1789. Of course, a wise man like Franklin knew that many other things are also certain. The Christian also knows that there are many certainties. Of spiritual truth, Christians are not afraid to say, "We know!" In fact, the word *know* occurs thirty-nine times in John's brief letter, eight times in this closing chapter.

Man has a deep desire for certainty, and he will even dabble in the occult in his effort to find out something for sure. A businessman having dinner with his pastor said to him, "Do you see those offices across the street? In them sit some of the most influential business leaders in this town. Many of them used to come over here regularly to consult a fortune-teller. She isn't here anymore, but a few years ago you could count up the millions of dollars in this room as men waited to consult her."

The life that is real is built on the divine certainties that are found in Jesus Christ. The world may accuse the Christian of being proud and dogmatic, but this does not keep him from saying, "I know!" In these closing verses of John's letter we find five Christian certainties on which we can build our lives with confidence.

## 1. Jesus Is God (5:6–10)

In 1 John 5:1–5, emphasis is placed on trusting Jesus Christ. A person who trusts Christ is born of God and is able to overcome the world. To believe that Jesus Christ is the Son of God is basic to Christian experience.

But how do we know that Jesus Christ is God? Some of His contemporaries called Him a liar and a deceiver (Matt. 27:63). Others have suggested He was a religious fanatic, a madman, or perhaps a Jewish patriot who was sincere but sadly mistaken. The people to whom John was writing were exposed to a popular false teaching that Jesus was merely a man on whom "the Christ" had come when Jesus was baptized. On the cross, "the Christ" left Jesus ("My God, my God, why hast thou forsaken me?"), and so He died like any other human being.

John's epistle refutes this false teaching. It presents three infallible witnesses to prove that Jesus is God.

**(1) First witness—the water.** Jesus came "by water and blood." The water refers to His baptism in Jordan, when the Father spoke from heaven and said, "This is my beloved Son, in whom I am well pleased" (Matt. 3:13–17). At the same time the Spirit descended like a dove and rested on Him. This was the Father's attestation of His Son at the beginning of Jesus' ministry.

**(2) Second witness—the blood.** But the Father gave further witness as the time drew near for Jesus to die. He spoke audibly to Jesus from heaven, and said, "I have both glorified it [My name], and will glorify it again" (John 12:28). Furthermore, the Father witnessed in miracle power when Jesus was on the cross: the supernatural darkness, the earthquake, and the rending of the temple veil (Matt. 27:45, 50–53). No wonder the centurion cried out, "Truly this was the Son of God!" (v. 54)

Jesus did not receive "the Christ" at His baptism and lose it at the cross. On both occasions, the Father witnessed to the deity of His Son.

**(3) Third witness—the Spirit.** The Spirit was given to bear witness to Christ (John 15:26; 16:14). We can trust the Spirit's witness because "the Spirit is truth." We were not present at the baptism of Christ or at His death, but the Holy Spirit was present. The Holy Spirit is the only Person active on earth today who was present when Christ was ministering here. The witness of the Father is past history, but the witness of the Spirit is present experience. The first is external, the second is internal—and both agree.

How does the Spirit witness within the heart of a believer? "For you have not received a spirit of slavery leading to fear again, but you have received a spirit of adoption as sons by which we cry out, 'Abba! Father!' The Spirit Himself testifies with our spirit that we are children of God" (Rom. 8:15–16 NASB). His witness is our inner confidence that we belong to Christ—not a confidence that we "work up" for ourselves, but a confidence that God gives us.

The Spirit also witnesses to us through the Word. As we read God's Word, He speaks to us and teaches us. This is not true of an unsaved man (1 Cor. 2:14); it is true only of a believer.

A Christian feels "at home" with God's people because the Spirit dwells in him. This is another way the Spirit bears witness.

The law required two or three witnesses for a matter to be settled (Deut. 19:15). The Father witnessed at the baptism and at the cross, and the Spirit witnesses today within the believer. The Spirit, the water, and the blood settle the matter: Jesus is God.

(Most scholars agree that 1 John 5:7 of the Authorized Version does not belong in the letter, but omitting it does not affect the teaching at all.)

We receive the witness of men, so why should we reject the witness of God?

People often say, "I wish I could have faith!" But everybody lives by faith! All day long, people trust one another. They trust the doctor and the pharmacist; they trust the cook in the restaurant; they even trust the fellow driving in the other lane on the highway. If we can trust men, why can we not trust God? And not to trust Him is to make Him a liar!

Jesus is God: This is the first Christian certainty, and it is foundational to everything else.

## 2. BELIEVERS HAVE ETERNAL LIFE (5:11–13)

The key word in 1 John 5:6–10 is *witness*, sometimes translated "record" or "testifieth." God gave witness to His Son, but He has also given witness to His sons—to individual believers. We know that we have eternal life! Not only is there the witness of the Spirit within; but there is also the witness of the Word of God. "These things I have written to you who believe in the name of the Son of God, so that you may know that you have eternal life" (1 John 5:13 NASB).

Eternal life is a gift; it is not something that we earn (John 10:27–29; Eph. 2:8–9). But this gift is a Person—Jesus Christ. We receive eternal life not only from Christ, but in Christ. "He who has the Son has the life" (1 John 5:12 NASB). Not just "life" but "the life"—the life "which is life indeed" (1 Tim. 6:19 NASB).

This gift is received by faith. God has gone on record in His Word as offering eternal life to those who will believe on Jesus Christ. Millions of Christians have proved that God's record is true. Not to believe it is to make God a liar. And if God is a liar, nothing is certain.

God wants His children to know that they belong to Him. John was inspired by the Spirit to write his gospel to assure us that "Jesus is the Christ, the Son of God" (John 20:31). He wrote this epistle so that we may be sure that we are the children of God (1 John 5:2, 19).

It would be helpful at this point to review the characteristics of God's children:

- "Everyone also who practices righteousness is born of Him" (1 John 2:29 NASB).

- "No one who is born of God practices sin" (1 John 3:9 NASB).
- "We know that we have passed out of death into life, because we love the brethren" (1 John 3:14 NASB).
- "Beloved, let us love one another, for love is from God; and everyone who loves is born of God and knows God" (1 John 4:7 NASB).
- "For whatsoever is born of God overcometh the world" (1 John 5:4).

If you bear these "birthmarks," you can say with confidence that you are a child of God.

When Sir James Simpson, the discoverer of chloroform, was on his deathbed, a friend asked him, "Sir, what are your speculations?"

Simpson replied, "Speculations! I have no speculations! 'For I know whom I have believed, and am persuaded that he is able to keep that which I have committed unto him against that day'" (2 Tim. 1:12).

### 3. GOD ANSWERS PRAYER (5:14–15)

It is one thing to know that Jesus is God and that we are God's children, but what about the needs and problems of daily life? Jesus helped people when He was here on earth; does He still help them? Earthly fathers take care of their children; does the heavenly Father respond when His children call on Him?

Christians have confidence in prayer, just as they have confidence as they await the judgment (1 John 2:28; 4:17). As we have seen, the word *confidence* means "freedom of speech." We can come to the Father freely and tell Him our needs.

Of course, there are conditions we must meet.

First, we must have a heart that does not condemn us (1 John 3:21–22). Unconfessed sin is a serious obstacle to answered prayer (Ps. 66:18). It is worth noting that differences between a Christian husband and his wife can hinder their prayers (1 Peter 3:1–7). If there is anything between us and any other Christian, we must settle it (Matt. 5:23–25). And unless a believer is abiding in Christ, in love and obedience, his prayers will not be answered (John 15:7).

Second, we must pray in God's will. "Thy will be done" (Matt. 6:10). "Prayer is a mighty instrument, not for getting man's will done in heaven, but for getting God's will done on earth," wrote Robert Law. George Mueller, who fed thousands of orphans with food provided in answer to prayer, said, "Prayer is not overcoming God's reluctance. It is laying hold of God's willingness."

There are times when we can only pray, "Not my will but thine be done," because we simply do not know God's will in a matter. But most of the time we can determine God's will by reading the Word, listening to the Spirit (Rom. 8:26–27), and discerning the circumstances around us. Our very faith to ask God for something is often proof that He wants to give it (Heb. 11:1).

There are many promises in the Bible that we can claim in prayer. God has promised to supply our needs (Phil. 4:19)—not our greeds! If we are obeying His will and really need something, He will supply it in His way and in His time.

"But if it is God's will for me to have a thing, then why should I pray about it?" Because prayer is the way God wants His children to get what they need. God not only ordains the end, but He also ordains the means to the end—prayer. And the more you think about it, the more wonderful this arrangement becomes. Prayer is really the thermometer of the spiritual life. God has ordained that I maintain a close walk with Him if I expect Him to meet my needs.

John did not write, "we shall have the requests," but, "we know that we have the requests" (1 John 5:15 NASB). The verb is present tense. We may not see the answer to a prayer immediately, but we have inner confidence that God has answered. This confidence, or faith, is "the evidence of things not seen" (Heb. 11:1). It is God witnessing to us that He has heard and answered.

What breathing is to a physical man, prayer is to a spiritual man. If we do not pray, we "faint" (Luke 18:1). Prayer is not only the utterance of the lips; it is also the desire of the heart. "Pray without ceasing" (1 Thess. 5:17) does not mean that a Christian is always saying an audible prayer. We are not heard for our "much speaking" (Matt. 6:7). No, "Pray without ceasing" suggests the attitude of the heart as well as the words of the lips. A Christian who has his heart fixed on Christ and is trying to glorify Him is praying constantly even when he is not conscious of it.

Famous preacher Charles Spurgeon was working hard on a message but was unable to complete it. It grew late and his wife said, "Why don't you go to bed. I'll wake you up early and you can finish your sermon in the morning."

Spurgeon dozed off and in his sleep began to preach the sermon that was giving him so much trouble! His wife wrote down what he said and the next morning gave her preacher-husband the notes.

"Why, that's exactly what I wanted to say!" exclaimed the surprised preacher. The message had been in his heart; it had simply needed expression. So with prayer: If we are abiding in Christ, the very desires of our hearts are heard by God whether we voice them or not.

The pages of the Bible and the pages of history are filled with reports of answered prayer. Prayer is not spiritual self-hypnosis. Nor do we pray because it makes us feel better. We pray because God has commanded us to pray and because prayer is the God-appointed means for a believer to receive what God wants to give him. Prayer keeps a Christian in the will of God, and living in the will of God keeps a Christian in the place of blessing and service. We are not beggars; we are children coming to a wealthy Father, who loves to give His children what they need.

Though He was God in the flesh, Jesus depended on prayer. He lived on earth, as we must, in dependence on the Father. He arose early in the morning to pray (Mark 1:35), though He had been up late the night before healing the multitudes. He sometimes spent all night in prayer (Luke 6:12).

In the garden of Gethsemane, He prayed with "strong crying and tears" (Heb. 5:7). On the cross He prayed three times. If the sinless Son of God needed to pray, how much more do we?

The most important thing about prayer is the will of God. We must take time to ascertain what God's will is in a matter, especially searching in the Bible for promises or principles that apply to our situation. Once we know the will of God, we can pray with confidence and then wait for Him to reveal the answer.

## 4. CHRISTIANS DO NOT PRACTICE SIN (5:16–19)

"We know that no one who is born of God sins" (1 John 5:18 NASB). "No one who is born of God practices sin" (3:9 NASB). Occasional sins are not here in view, but habitual sins, the practice of sin. Because a believer has a new nature ("God's seed," v. 9), he has new desires and appetites and is not interested in sin.

A Christian faces three enemies, all of which want to lead him into sin: the world, the flesh, and the Devil.

The world "lies in the power of the evil one" (1 John 5:19 NASB), Satan—the god of this age (2 Cor. 4:3–4, literal translation) and the prince of this world (John 14:30). He is the spirit who works in the children of disobedience (Eph. 2:2).

Satan has many devices for leading a believer into sin. He tells lies, as he did to Eve (Gen. 3; 2 Cor. 11:1–3), and when men believe his lies, they turn away from and disobey God's truth. Or, Satan may inflict physical suffering, as he did with Job and Paul (2 Cor. 12:7–9). In David's case, Satan used pride as his weapon and urged David to number the people and in this way defy God (1 Chron. 21). Satan is like a serpent who deceives (Rev. 12:9) and a lion who devours (1 Peter 5:8–9). He is a formidable enemy.

Then there is the problem of the flesh, the old nature with which we were born and that is still with us. True, we have a new nature (the divine seed, 1 John 3:9) within us, but we do not always yield to our new nature.

The world is our third enemy (1 John 2:15, 17). It is easy for us to yield to the desires of the flesh, the desires of the eyes, and the pride of life! The atmosphere around us makes it hard for us to keep our minds pure and our hearts true to God.

Then how does a believer keep from sinning?

First John 5:18 gives the answer: Jesus Christ keeps the believer so that the enemy cannot get his hands on him. "He [Christ] who was born of God keeps him [the believer], and the evil one does not touch him" (NASB). The Authorized Version here gives the impression that a believer keeps himself from sin, but this is not what the verse says. Of course, it is true that a Christian must keep himself in the love of God (Jude 21), but it is not true that a Christian must depend on himself to overcome Satan.

Peter's experience with Satan helps us to understand this truth.

"Simon, Simon," said Jesus, "behold, Satan has demanded permission to sift you like wheat; but I have prayed for you, that your faith may not fail; and you, when once you have turned again, strengthen your brothers" (Luke 22:31–32 NASB).

To begin with, Satan cannot touch any believer without God's permission. Satan wanted to sift all the disciples, and Jesus gave him permission. But Jesus prayed especially for Peter, and His prayer was answered. Peter's faith did not ultimately fail, even though his courage failed. Peter was restored and became a mighty and effective soul winner.

Whenever Satan attacks us, we can be sure that God gave him permission. And if God gave him permission He will also give us power to overcome, because God will never permit us to be tested above our strength (1 Cor. 10:13).

One of the characteristics of "spiritual young men" is their ability to overcome the evil one (1 John 2:13–14). Their secret? "The word of God abides in you" (1 John 2:14 NASB). Part of the armor of God is the sword of the Spirit (Eph. 6:17), and this sword overcomes Satan.

When a believer sins, he can confess his sin and be forgiven (1 John 1:9). But a believer dare not play with sin, because sin is lawlessness (3:4, where "transgression of the law" means "lawlessness"). A person who practices sin proves that he belongs to Satan (vv. 7–10). Furthermore, God warns that sin can lead to physical death!

"All unrighteousness is sin," but some sin is worse than other sin. All sin is hateful to God, and should be hateful to a believer; but some sin is punished with death. John told us (1 John 5:16–17) about the case of a brother (a believer) whose life was taken because of sin.

The Bible mentions people who died because of their sin. Nadab and Abihu, the two sons of Aaron the priest, died because they deliberately disobeyed God (Lev. 10:1–7). Korah and his clan opposed God and died (Num. 16). Achan was stoned because he disobeyed Joshua's orders from God at Jericho (Josh. 6—7). A man named Uzzah touched the ark and God killed him (2 Sam. 6).

"But those are Old Testament examples!" someone may argue. "John was writing to New Testament believers, who live under grace!"

To whom much is given, much shall be required. A believer today has a far greater responsibility to obey God than did the Old Testament saints. We have a complete Bible, we have the full revelation of God's grace, and we have the Holy Spirit living within us to help us obey God. But there are cases in the New Testament of believers who lost their lives because they disobeyed God.

Ananias and Sapphira lied to God about their offering, and they both died (Acts 5:1–11). Some believers at Corinth died because of the way they had acted at the Lord's Supper (1 Cor. 11:30). And 1 Corinthians 5:1–5 suggests that a certain offender would have died had he not repented and confessed his sin (2 Cor. 2:6–8).

If a believer does not judge, confess, and forsake sin, God must chasten him. This process is described in Hebrews 12:1–13, which suggests that a person who does not subject himself to the Father will not live (v. 9). In other words, first God "spanks" his rebellious children, and if they do not yield to His will, He may remove them from the world lest their disobedience lead others astray and bring further disgrace to His name.

"The sin unto death" is not one specific sin. Rather, it is a kind of sin— it is the sort of sin that leads to death. With Nadab and Abihu, it was their presumption in taking the priest's office and entering the Holy of Holies. In the case of Achan it was covetousness. Ananias and Sapphira were guilty of hypocrisy and even of lying to the Holy Spirit.

If a Christian sees a brother committing sin, he should pray for him (1 John 5:16), asking that he confess his sin and return to fellowship with the Father. But if in his praying, he does not sense that he is asking in God's will (as instructed in 1 John 5:14–15), then he should not pray for the brother. "Therefore, pray not thou for this people, neither lift up cry nor prayer for them, neither make intercession to me: for I will not hear thee" (Jer. 7:16).

James 5:14–20 somewhat parallels 1 John 5:16–17. James described a believer who is sick, possibly because of his sin. He sends for the elders, who come to him and pray for him. The prayer of faith heals him, and if he has sinned his sins are forgiven. "The prayer of faith" is prayer in the will of God, as described in 1 John 5:14–15. It is "praying in the Holy Spirit" (Jude 20 NASB).

Christians do not deliberately practice sin. They have the divine nature within; Jesus Christ guards them, and they do not want God's discipline.

## 5. THE CHRISTIAN LIFE IS THE REAL LIFE (5:20–21)

Jesus Christ is the true God. We know Him who is true, and we are in Him who is true. We have "the real thing"!

"We know that our real life is in the true One, and in His Son, Jesus Christ. This is the real God and this is real, eternal life" (1 John 5:20 PH). Reality has been the theme throughout John's letter, and now we are reminded of it again.

John was probably writing to believers in the city of Ephesus, a city given over to the worship of idols. The temple of Diana, one of the wonders of the ancient world, was located in Ephesus, and the making and selling of idols was one of the chief occupations of the people there (Acts 19:21–41). Surrounded by idolatry, Christians there were under tremendous pressure to conform.

But "we know that there is no such thing as an idol in the world, and that there is no God but one" (1 Cor. 8:4 NASB). That is, "an idol has no real existence" (NASB, marg.). The tragedy of idolatry is that a dead image can do a worshipper no good because it is not genuine. Hebrew writers in the Old Testament called idols "nothings, vain things, vapors, emptiness." An idol is a lifeless, useless substitute for the real thing.

The Psalms contain caustic indictments of idolatry (Ps. 115:1–8; 135:15–18). To human vision, an idol looks real—eyes, ears, mouth, nose, hands, feet—but these are but useless imitations of the real thing. The eyes are blind, the ears are deaf, the mouth is silent, the hands and feet are paralyzed. But the real tragedy is that "those who make them will become like them, everyone who trusts in them" (v. 8 NASB). We become like the god we worship!

This is the secret of the life that is real. Because we have met the true God, through His Son Jesus Christ, we are in contact with reality. Our fellowship is with a God who is genuine. As we have seen, the word *real* means "the original as opposed to a copy" and "the authentic as opposed to an imitation." Jesus Christ is the true light (John 1:9), and true bread (John 6:32), and true vine (John 15:1), and truth itself (John 14:6). He is the Original; everything else is a copy. He is authentic; everything else is only an imitation.

Christians live in an atmosphere of reality. Most unsaved people live in an atmosphere of pretense and sham. Christians have been given spiritual discernment to know the true from the false, but the unsaved do not have this understanding. Christians do not simply choose between good and bad; they choose between true and false. An idol represents that which is false and empty; and a person who lives for idols will himself become false and empty.

Few people today bow to idols of wood and metal. Nevertheless, other idols capture their attention and affection. Covetousness, for example, is idolatry (Col. 3:5). A man may worship his bankbook or his stock portfolio just as fervently as a so-called heathen worships his ugly idol. "Thou shalt worship the Lord thy God, and him only shalt thou serve" (Matt. 4:10). The thing we serve is the thing we worship! Whatever controls our lives and "calls the signals" is our god.

This explains why God warns us against the sin of idolatry. Not only is it a violation of His commandment (Ex. 20:1–6), but it is also a subtle way for Satan to take control of us. When "things" take God's place in our lives, we are guilty of idolatry. This means we are living for the unreal instead of for the real.

To a man of the world, the Christian life is unreal and the worldly life is real. This is because a man of the world lives by what he sees and feels (things) and not by what God says in His Word. An idol is a temporal thing, Jesus Christ is eternal God. "For the things which are seen are temporal, but the things which are not seen are eternal" (2 Cor. 4:18 NASB).

Like Moses, a Christian endures "as seeing him who is invisible" (Heb. 11:27). Faith is "the evidence of things not seen" (Heb. 11:1). Noah had never seen a flood, yet by faith he "saw" it coming and did what God told him to do. Abraham "saw" a heavenly city and country by faith, and was willing to forsake his own earthly home to follow God. All of the great heroes of faith named in Hebrews 11 accomplished what they did because they "saw the invisible" by faith. In other words, they were in contact with reality.

The world boasts of its enlightenment, but a Christian walks in the real light because God is light. The world talks about love, but it knows nothing of the real love that a Christian experiences because "God is love." The world displays its wisdom and learning, but a Christian lives in truth because "the Spirit is truth." God is light, love, and truth, and these together make a life that is real.

"But it makes no difference what a man believes so long as he is sincere!"

This popular excuse hardly needs refutation. Does it make any difference what the pharmacist believes, or the surgeon, or the chemist? It makes all the difference in the world!

> Shed a tear for Jimmy Brown;
> Poor Jimmy is no more.
> For what he thought was $H_2O$*
> Was $H_2SO_4$![†]

A Christian has "turned to God from idols to serve the living and true God" (1 Thess. 1:9). Idols are dead, but Christ is the living God. Idols are false, but Christ is the true God. This is the secret of the life that is real!

So John's admonition, "Keep yourselves from idols," can be paraphrased, "Watch out for the imitation and the artificial and be real!"

* Water

† Sulfuric acid

# QUESTIONS FOR PERSONAL REFLECTION
# OR GROUP DISCUSSION

1. From this passage, Wiersbe draws out five Christian absolutes on which we can build our lives. Explain each absolute in your own words.

2. What is the significance of "water and blood" (1 John 5:6)?

3. How does the Holy Spirit witness of Jesus to believers?

4. God hears us if we pray according to His will (v. 14). How can we know what is according to His will?

5. If God already knows our needs and wants to fulfill them, why do we need to pray about them?

6. How is prayer the "thermometer of the spiritual life"?

7. How did Jesus show that He depended on prayer? Give examples.

8. How does Satan lead believers into sin?

9. How does God protect believers from sin?

10. "Christians live in an atmosphere of reality. Most unsaved people live in an atmosphere of pretense and sham." Do you agree? Explain.

11. How do you feel differently about being a Christian in today's world after studying 1 John?

# The "BE" series . . .

For years pastors and lay leaders have embraced Warren W. Wiersbe's very accessible commentary of the Bible through the individual "BE" series. Through the work of David C. Cook Global Mission, the "BE" series is part of a library of books made available to indigenous Christian workers. These are men and women who are called by God to grow the kingdom through their work with the local church worldwide. Here are a few of their remarks as to how Dr. Wiersbe's writings have benefited their ministry.

"Most Christian books I see are priced too high for me . . . I received a collection that included 12 Wiersbe commentaries a few months ago and I have read every one of them.
I use them for my personal devotions every day and they are incredibly helpful for preparing sermons.
The contribution David C. Cook is making to the church in India is amazing."

—Pastor E. M. Abraham, Hyderabad, India

# Get the Entire
# Fifty-Book "BE" Series
## in Two Volumes

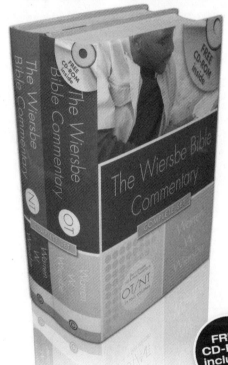